MANDALA:
Calming and stress relieving patterns

By: Rashmi Makwana

The book provides 40 colouring patterns in form of Mandala. All the design illustrations are unique and detailed. covering a range of patterns from modern abstract geometrical form to more basic pattern form.

Mandala means "circle". It is a geometric configuration with various shapes, symbols and lines. Various religious and spiritual exercises may use mandala to focus and creating a spiritual guidance tool. It may be used to aid the meditation state. A mandala represents a spiritual journey, starting from outside moving towards the inner core through various layers.

Carl Jung, in his studies claimed that mandala corresponds to the inner situation of the person, gradually discovering that mandala is the self, wholeness of the personality, which if all goes well is harmonious. he claimed that mandala emerges during moments of intense personal growth. it serves a conservative purpose of restoring previously existing order. It is an ascending spiral of creativity and growth, which grows upward simultaneously returning to the core again and again. Transpersonal psychologist David Fontana proposed that the symbolic nature of a mandala may help one "to access progressively deeper levels of the unconscious, ultimately assisting the meditator to experience a mystical sense of oneness with the ultimate unity from which the cosmos in all its manifold forms arises."

Mandalas have been part of history and many religious sects such as Hinduism, Buddhism, Christianity, Aztec and Mayan. Proving its merit to humans again and again. we have used mandalas as the form of life in art, architecture, representation in science, in archaeology and in politics. Mandalas are present everywhere in from of designs, pattern or a higher message.

At end of the book, there are ten blank pages to create you own mandalas showcasing your true self. Guiding your mind into being who you are. Feeling the feelings of self-worth and self-love to create the geometry of your state of mind.

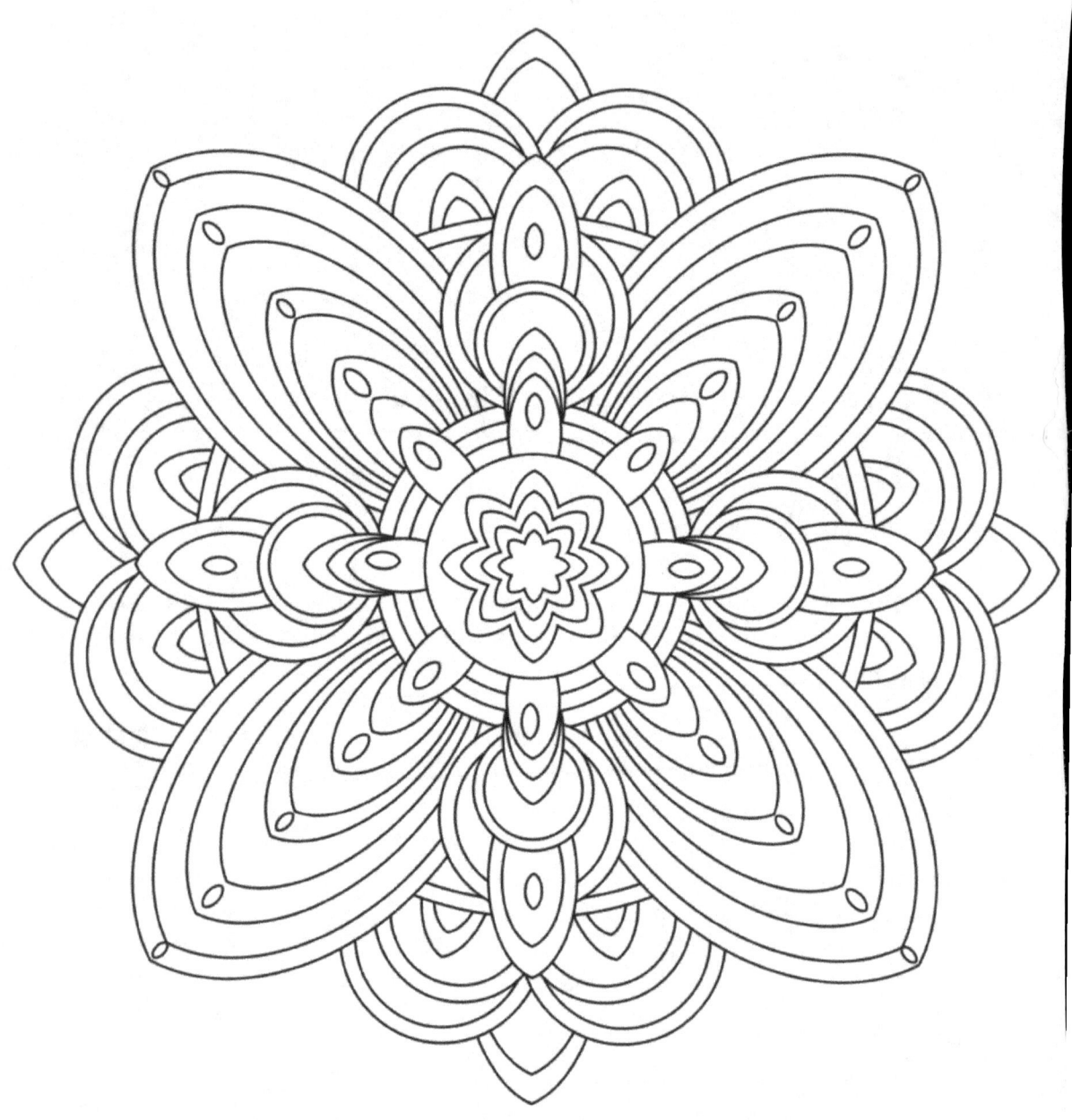

"There is no path to happiness; happiness is the path."- Buddha

Today I am grateful for _____

_____

_____

_____

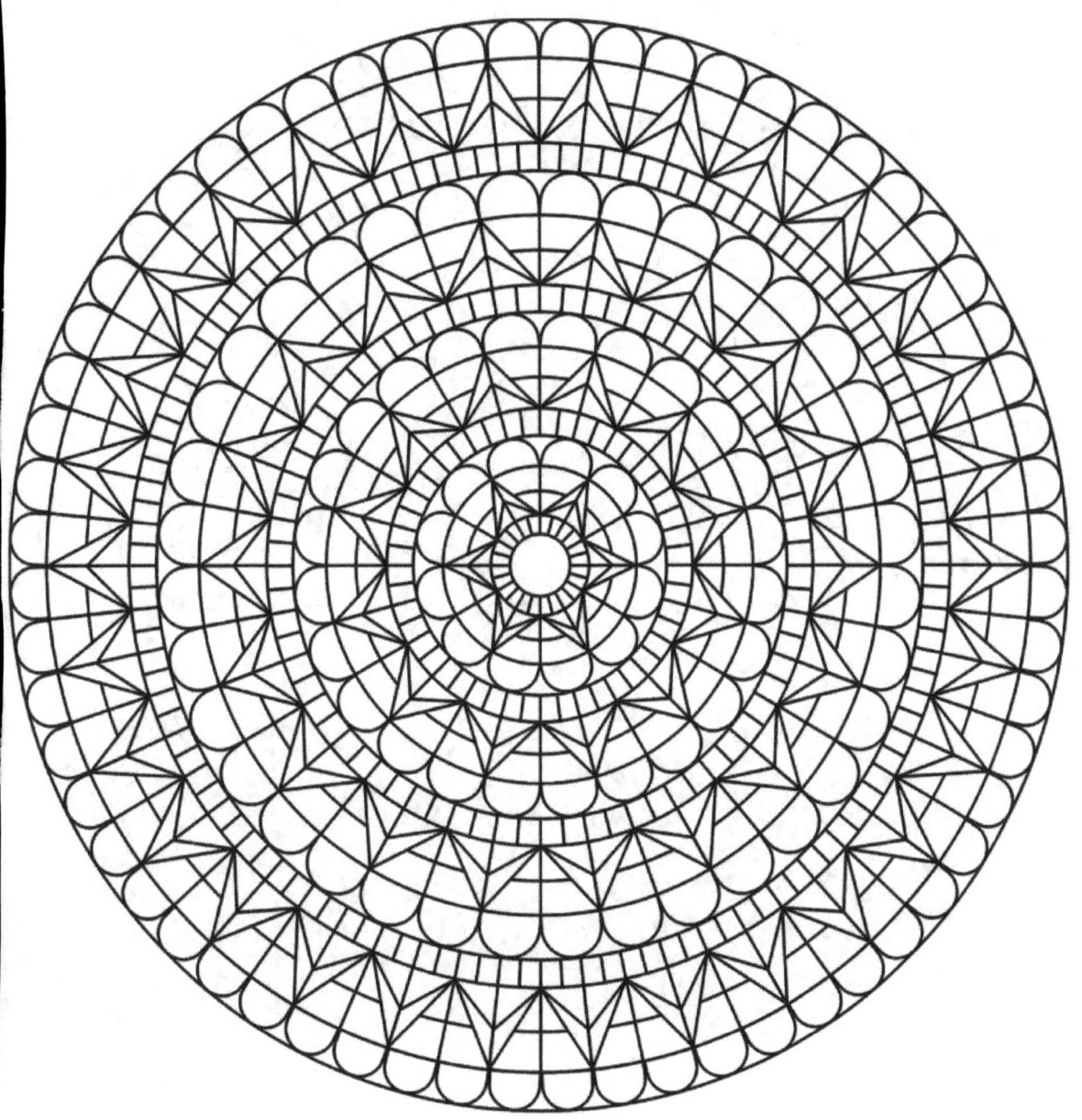

"I, not events, have the power to make me happy or unhappy today. I can choose which it shall be. Yesterday is dead, tomorrow hasn't arrived yet. I have just one day, today, and I'm going to be happy in it." —Groucho Marx

Today I am grateful for _____

_____

_____

_____

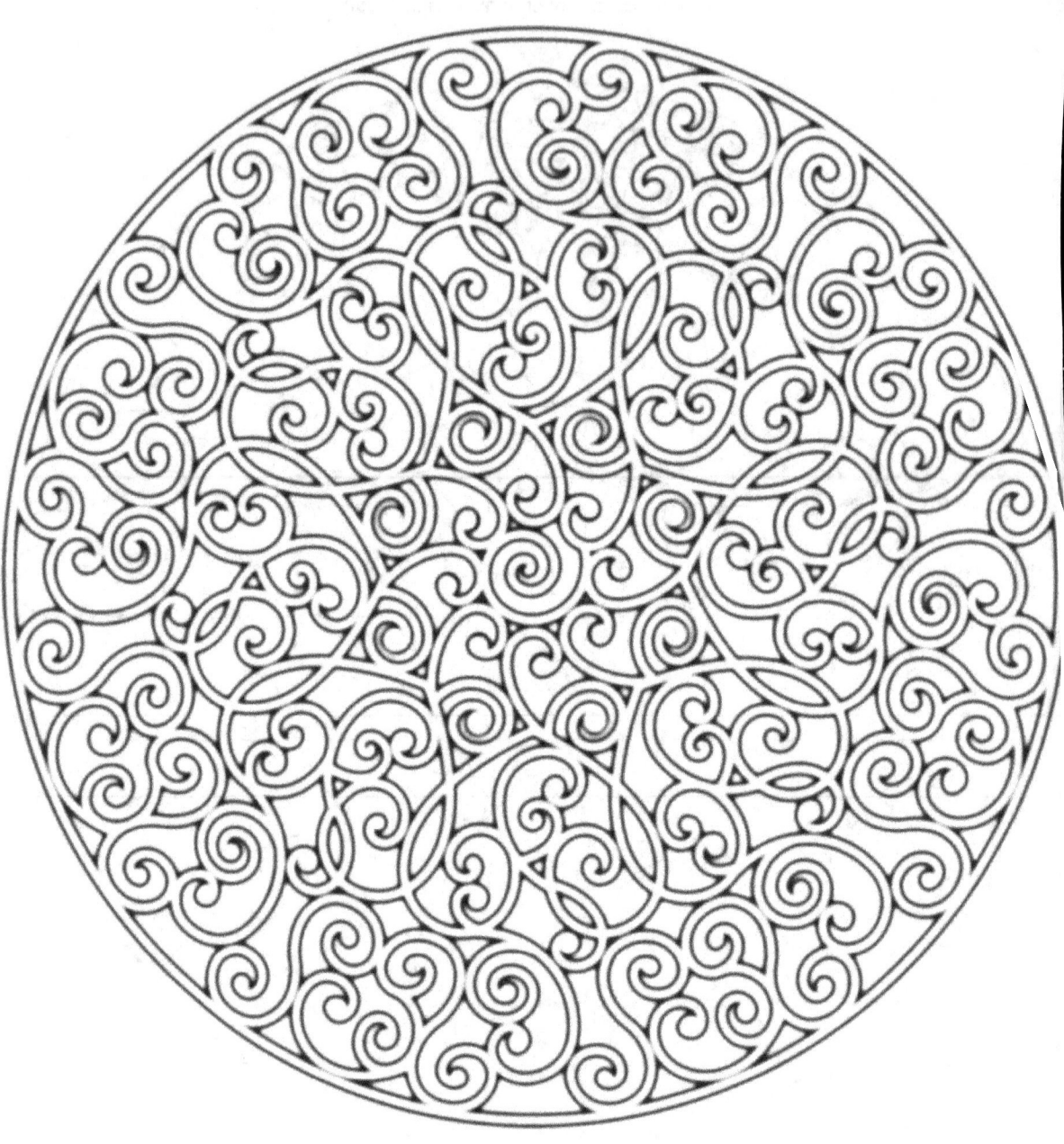

"I have chosen to be happy because it's good for my health." – Voltaire

Today I am grateful for

_____

_____

_____

_____

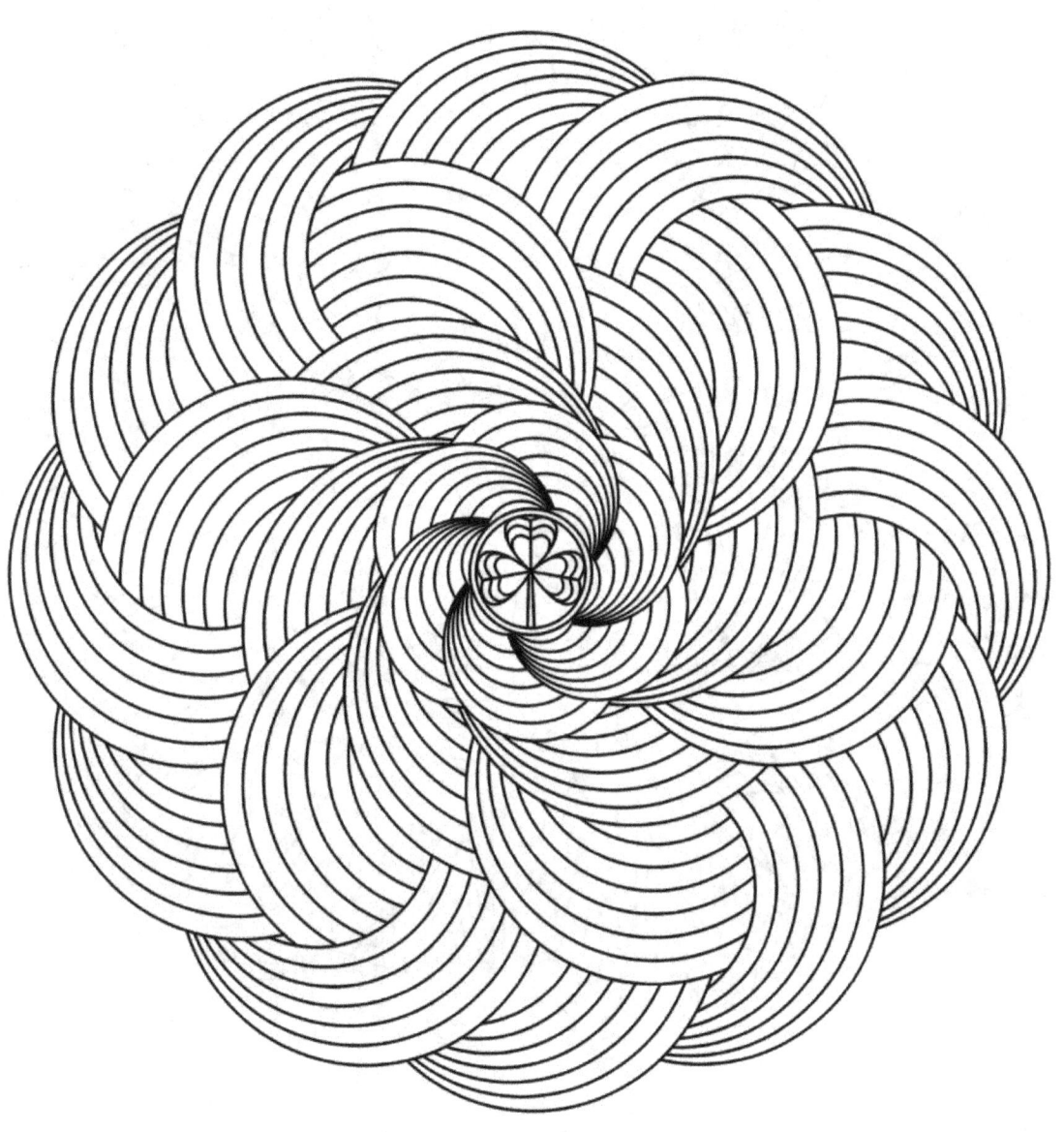

"Happiness is a journey, not a destination."- Buddha

Today I am grateful for _____

_____

_____

_____

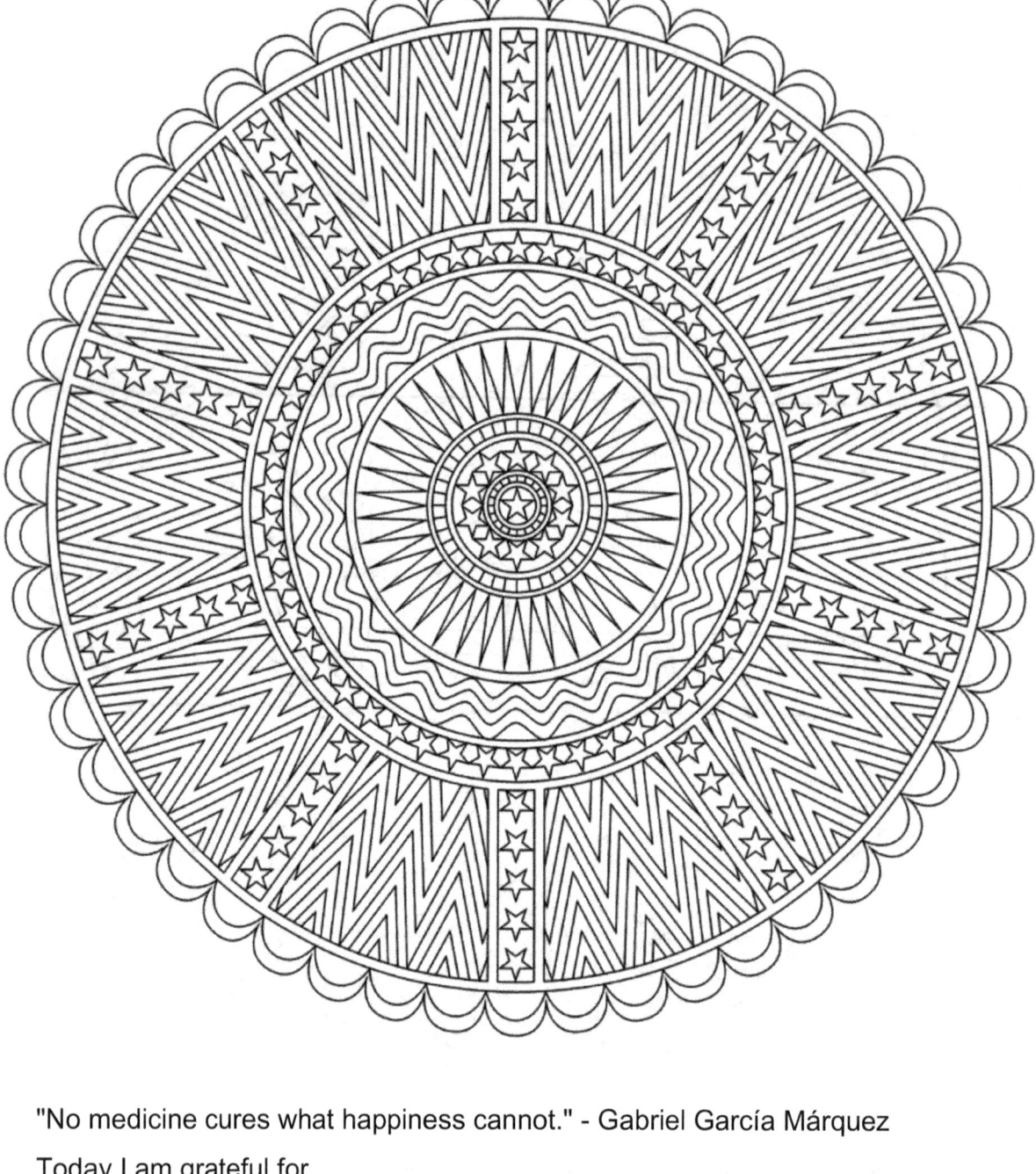

"No medicine cures what happiness cannot." - Gabriel García Márquez

Today I am grateful for _____

_____

_____

_____

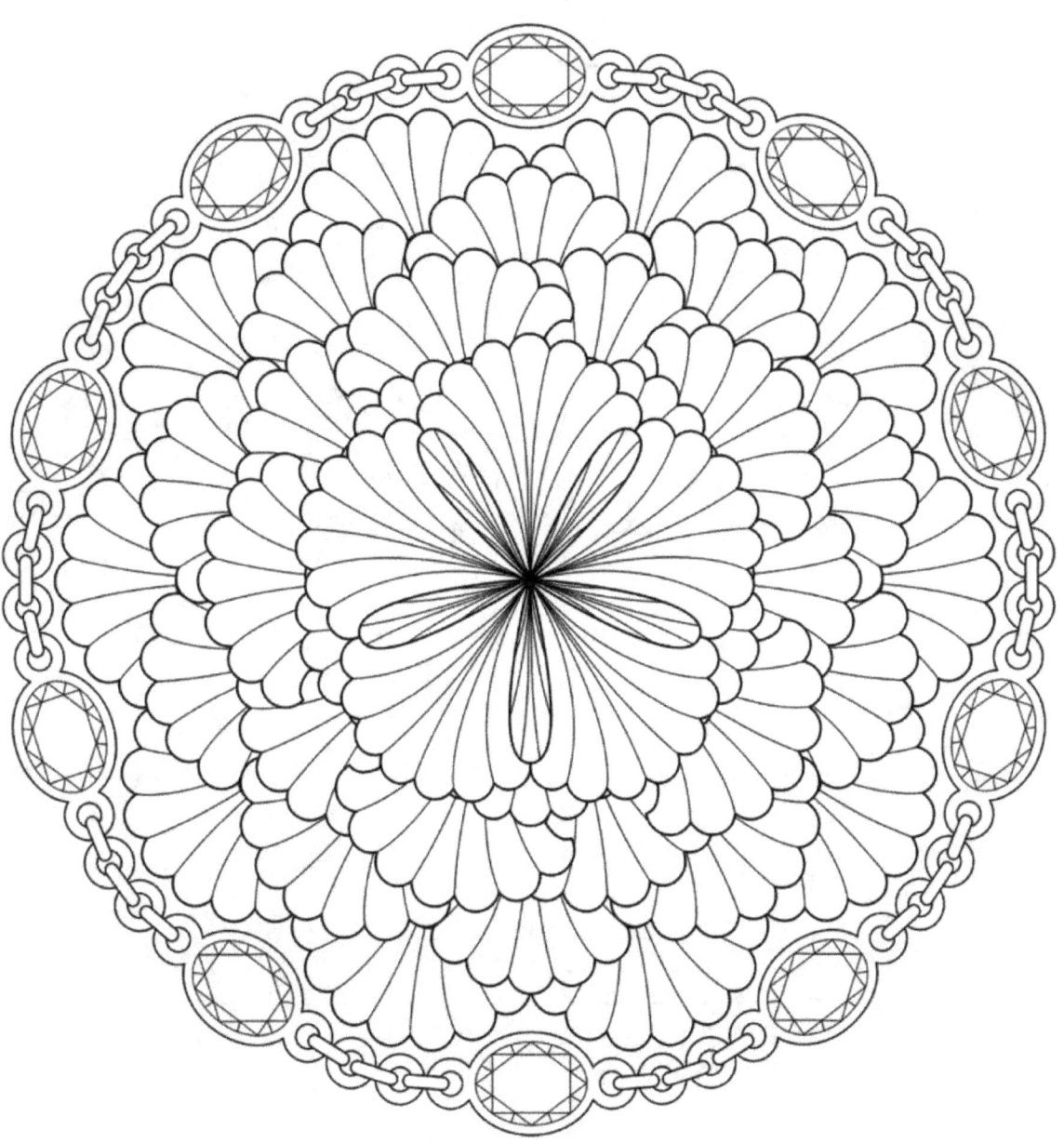

"They say a person needs just three things to be truly happy in this world: Someone to love, something to do, and something to hope for." - Tom Bodett

Today I am grateful for _____

_____

_____

_____

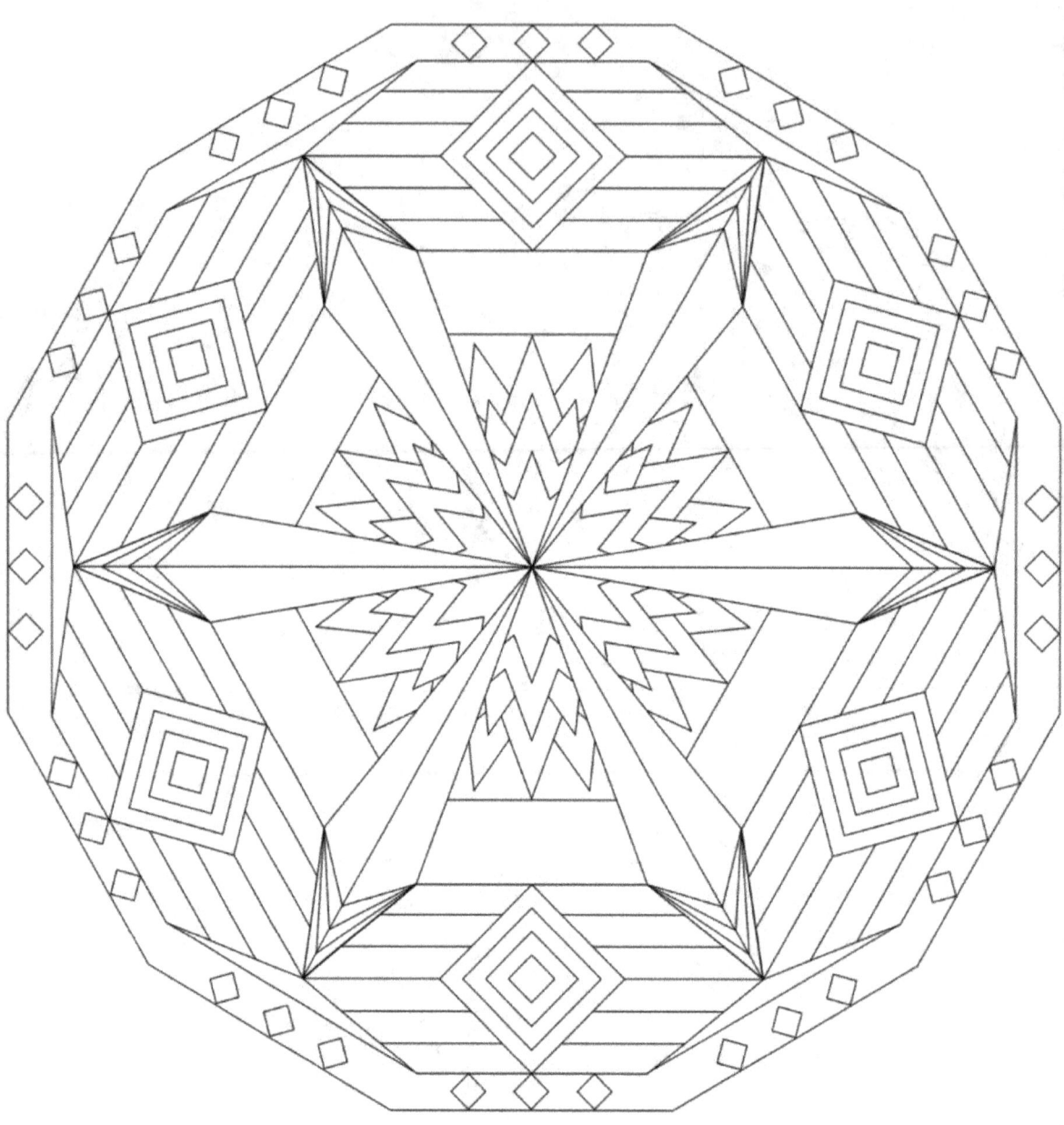

"Let us be grateful to the people who make us happy; they are the charming gardeners who make our souls blossom." - Marcel Proust

Today I am grateful for _____

_____

_____

_____

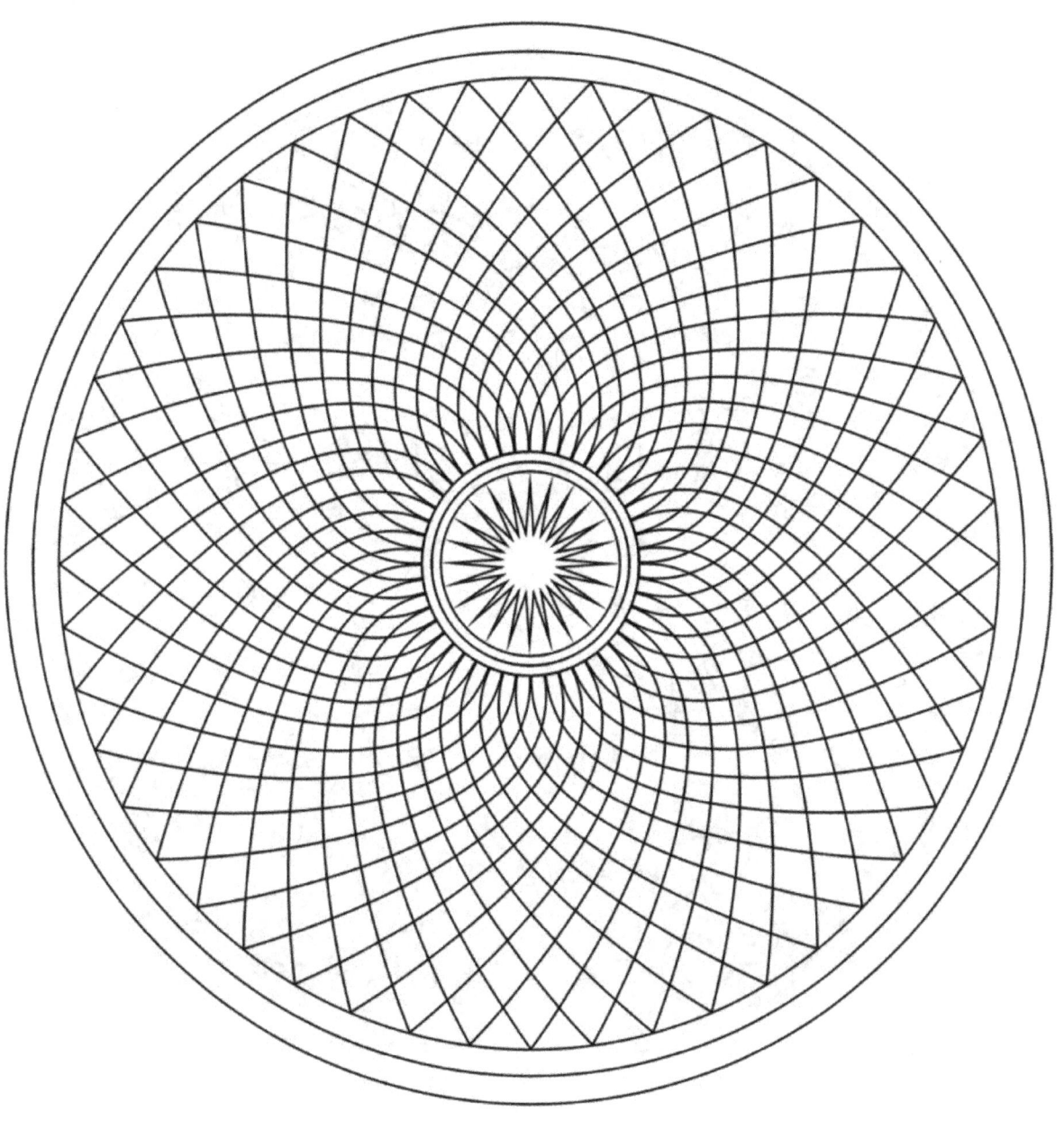

"Happiness is a warm puppy." - Charles M. Schulz

Today I am grateful for _____

_____

_____

_____

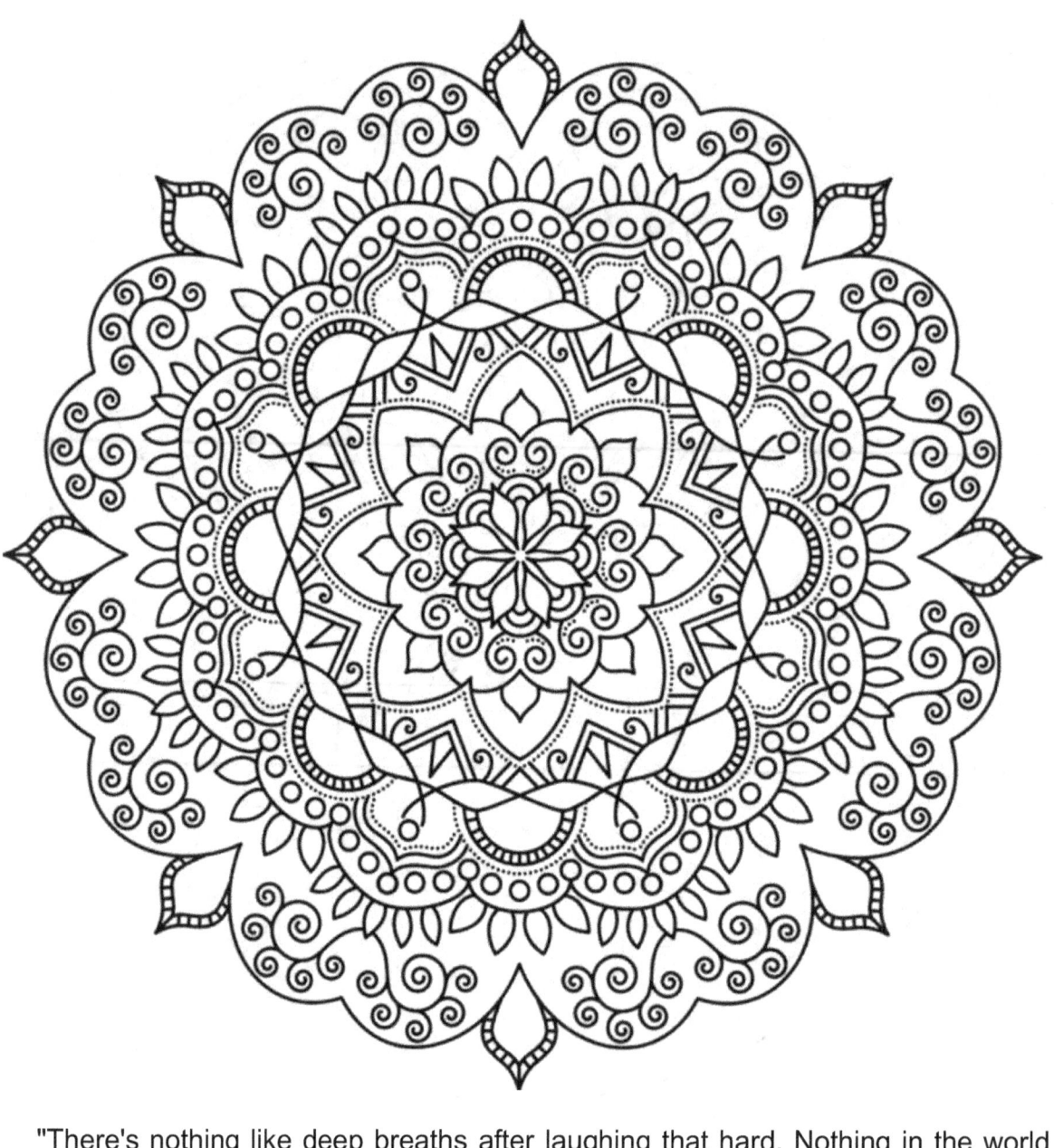

"There's nothing like deep breaths after laughing that hard. Nothing in the world like a sore stomach for the right reasons." - Stephen Chbosky, 'The Perks of Being a Wallflower'

Today I am grateful for _____

_____

_____

_____

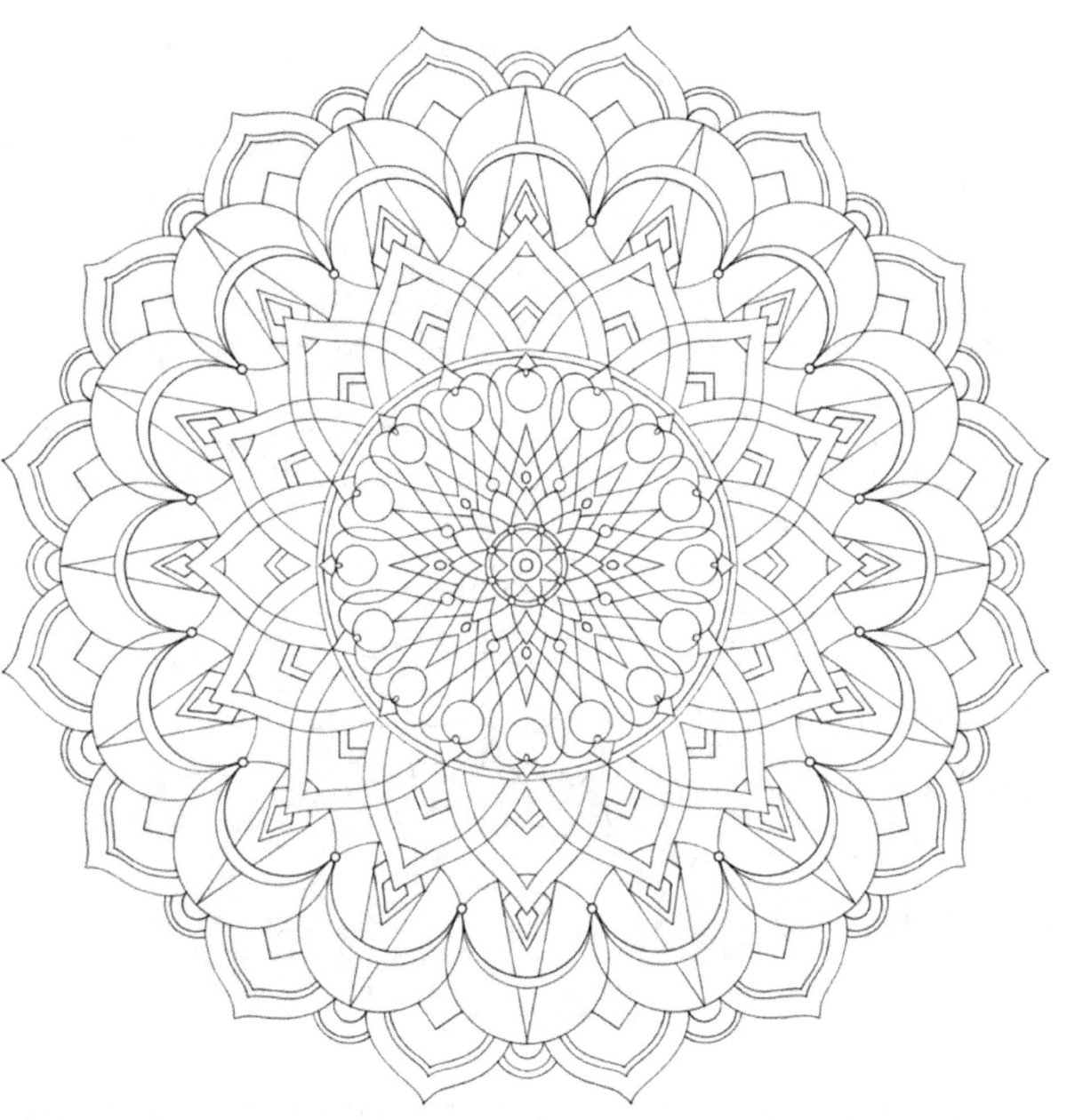

"Sanity and happiness are an impossible combination."- Mark Twain

Today I am grateful for _____

_____

_____

_____

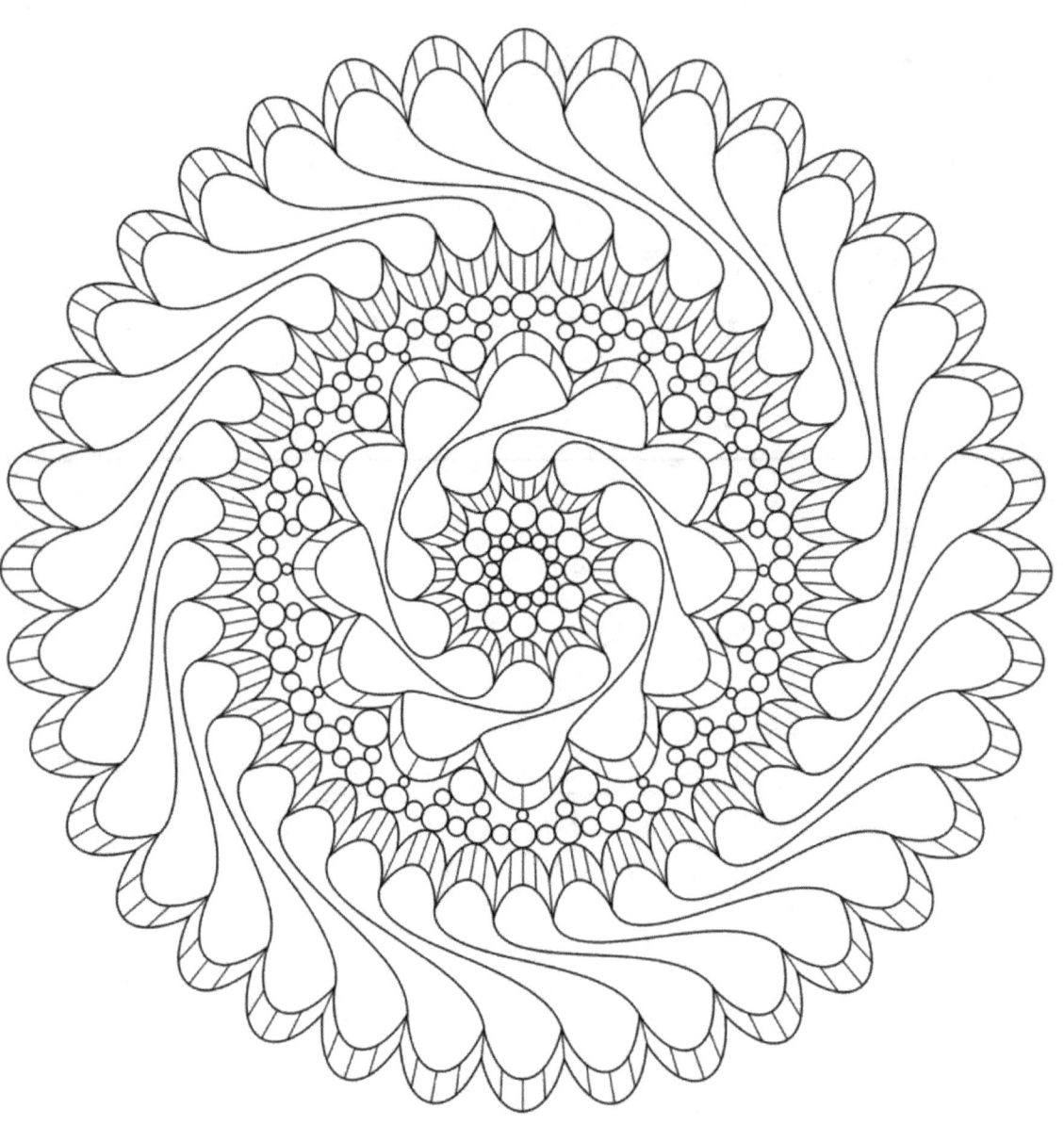

"It's so hard to forget pain, but it's even harder to remember sweetness. We have no scar to show for happiness. We learn so little from peace."- Chuck Palahniuk, 'Diary'

Today I am grateful for _____

_____

_____

_____

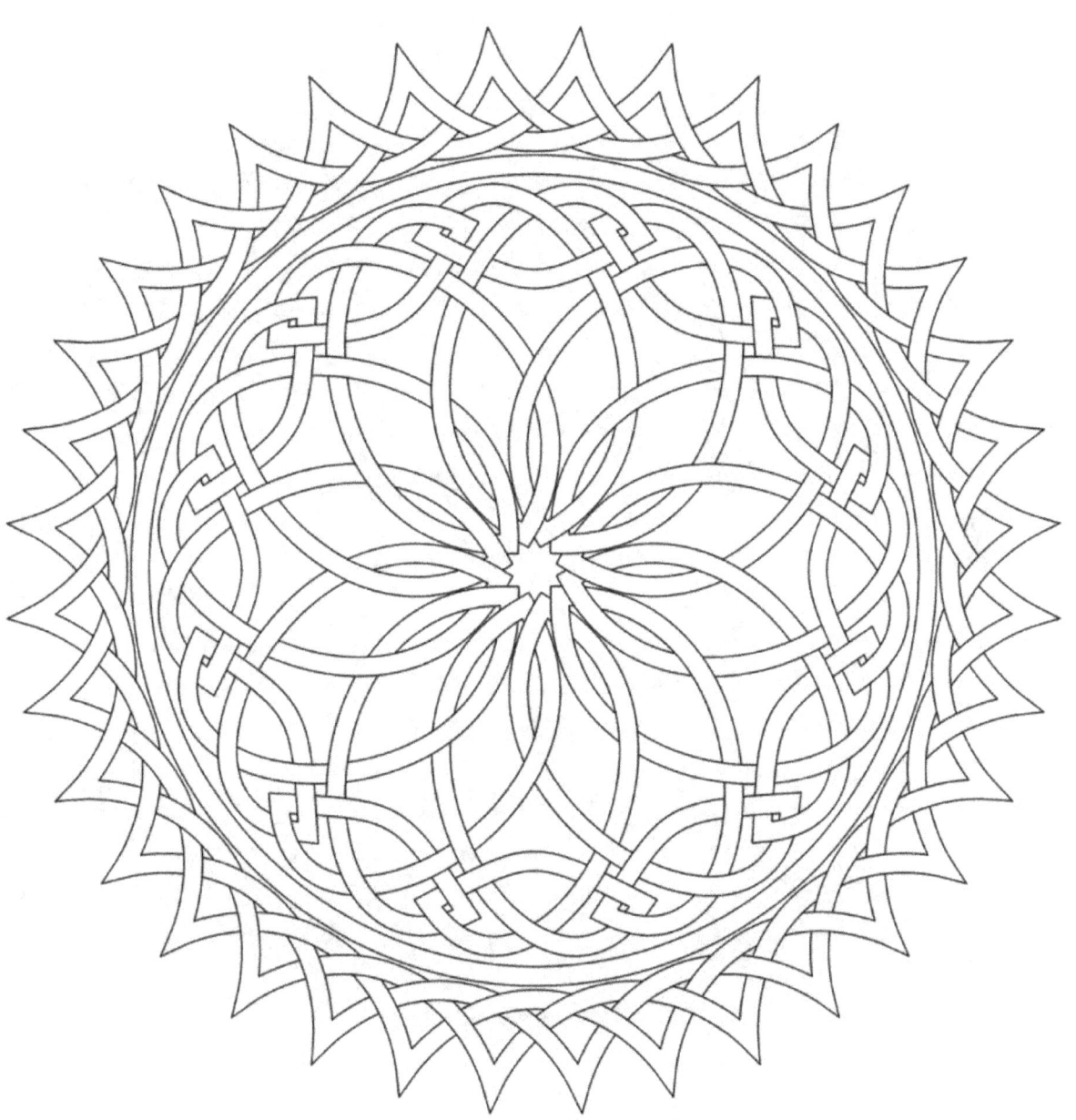

"If you want to be happy, do not dwell in the past, do not worry about the future, focus on living fully in the present."- Roy T. Bennett

Today I am grateful for _____

_____

_____

_____

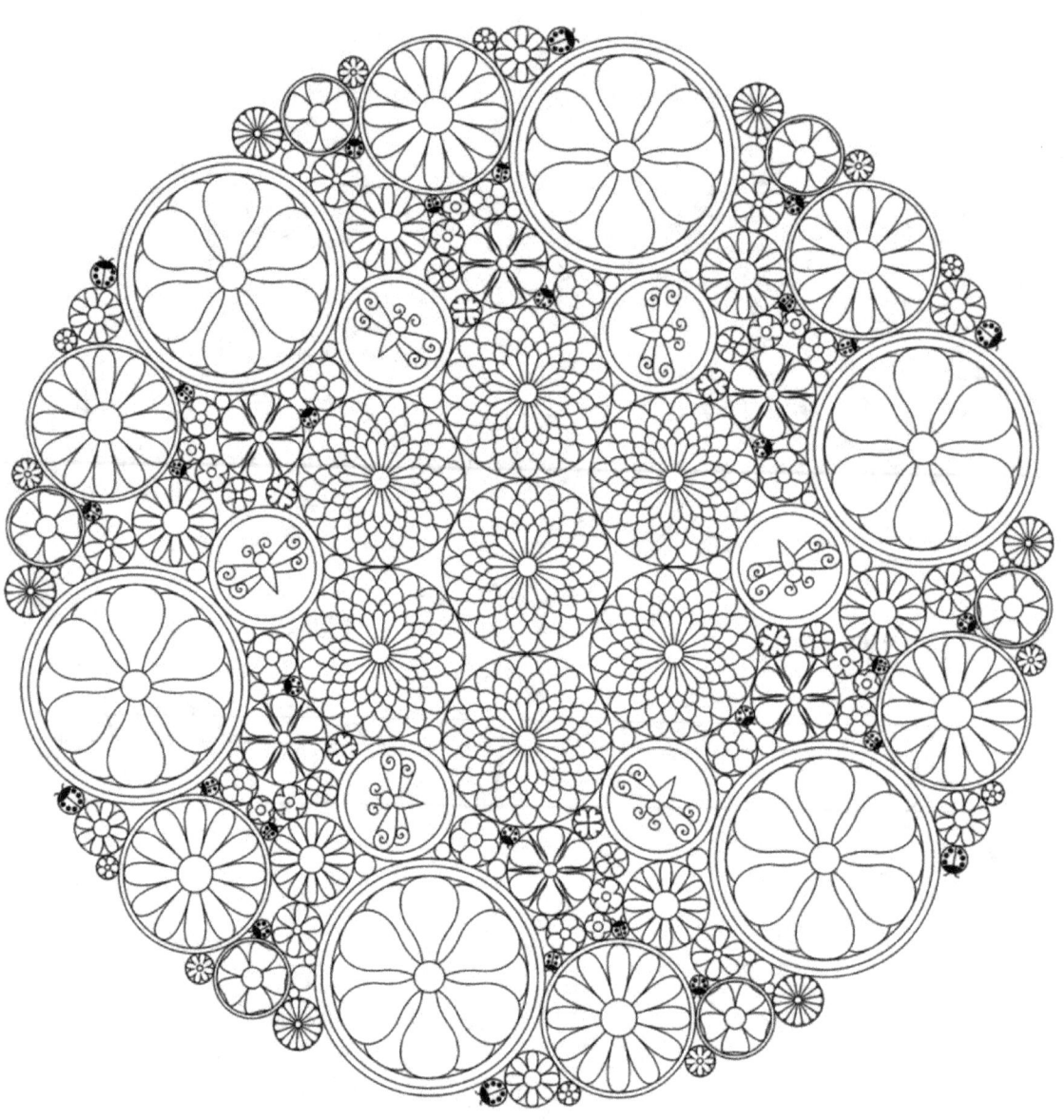

"It isn't what you have or who you are or where you are or what you are doing that makes you happy or unhappy. It is what you think about it." - Dale Carnegie

Today I am grateful for _____

_____

_____

_____

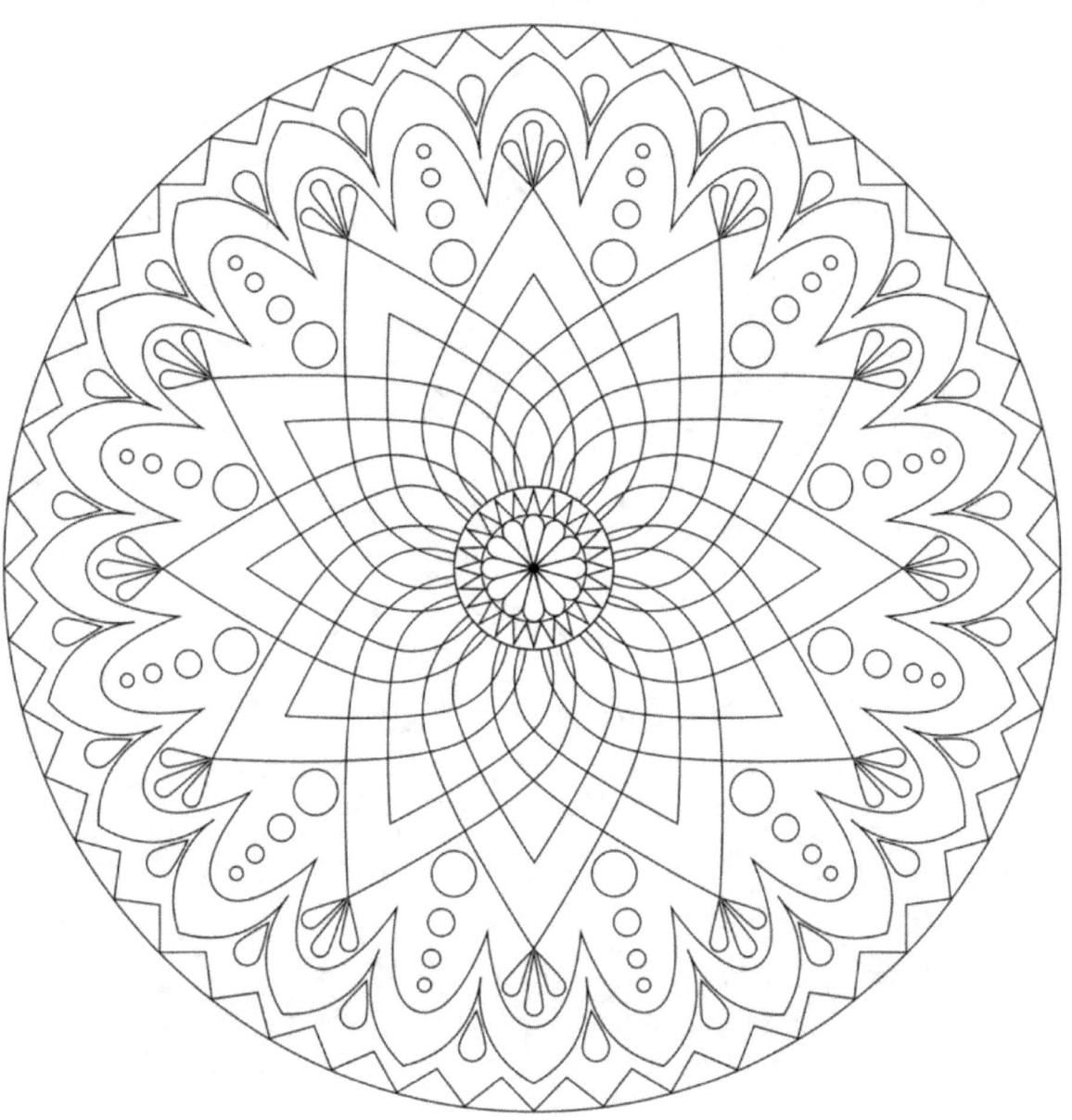

"Happiness is a state of mind. It's just according to the way you look at things." - Walt Disney

Today I am grateful for _____

_____

_____

_____

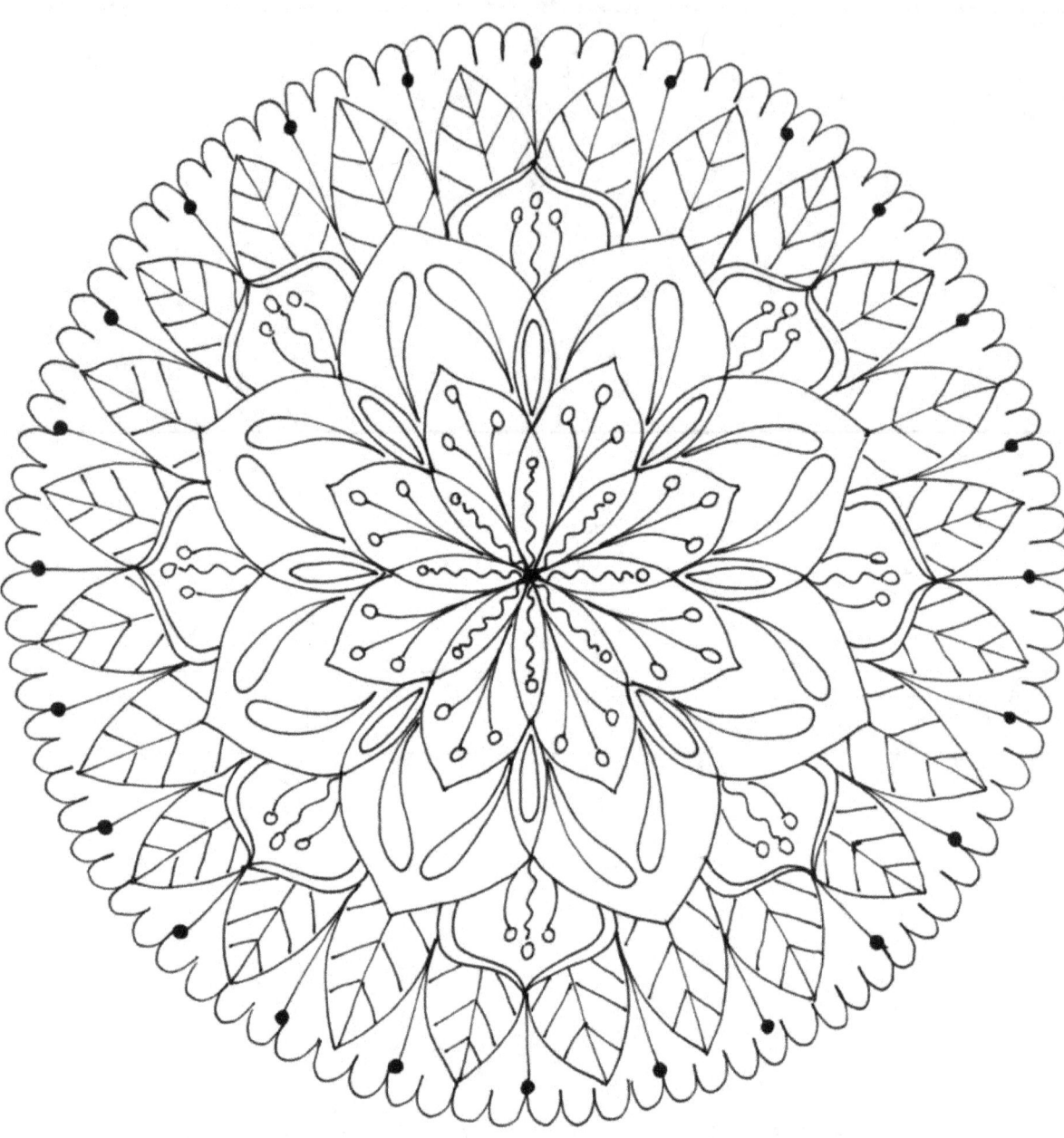

"Think of all the beauty still left around you and be happy." - Anne Frank

Today I am grateful for

_____

_____

_____

_____

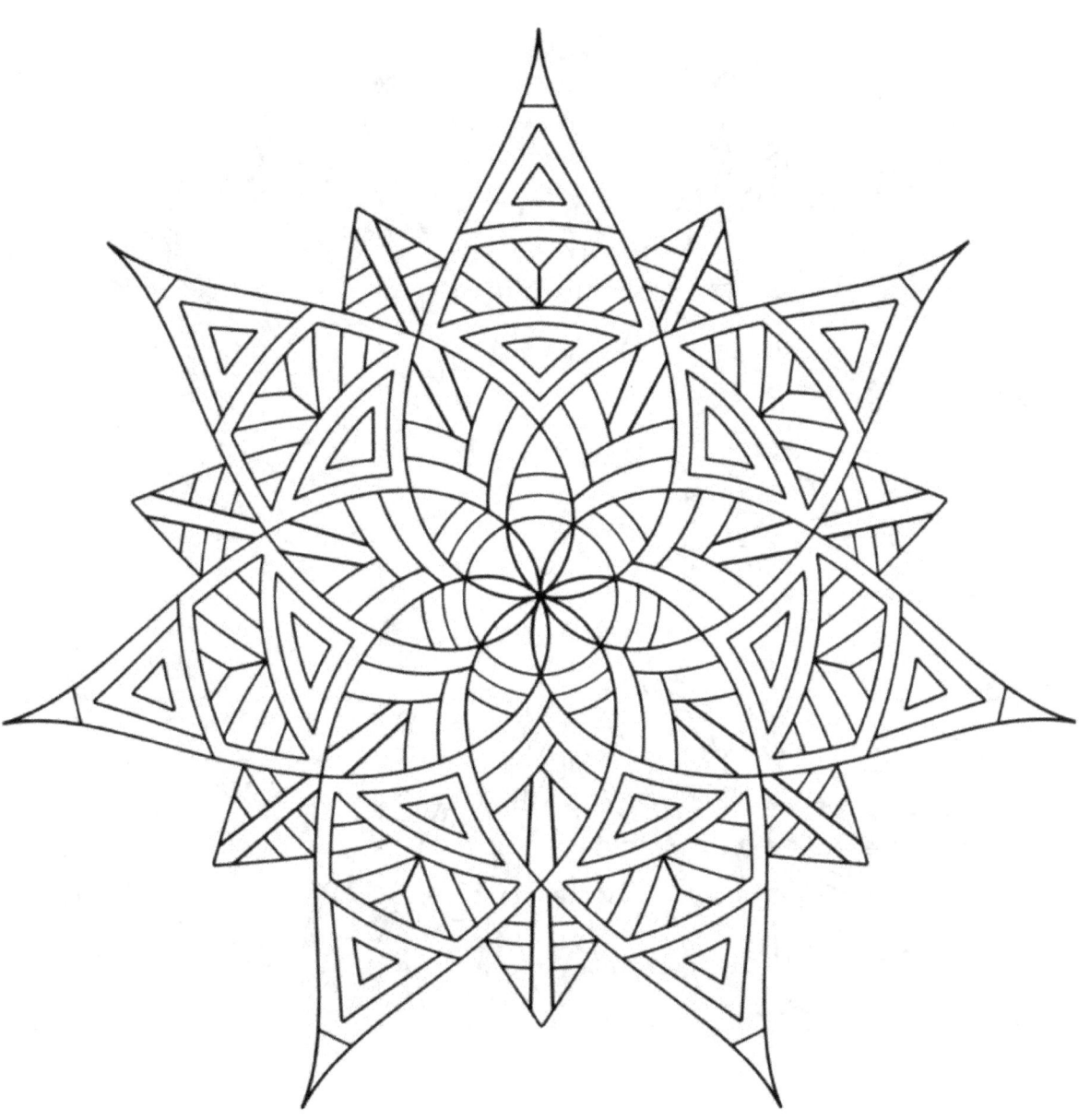

"Happiness is not a goal...it's a by-product of a life well-lived." - Eleanor Roosevelt

Today I am grateful for _____

_____

_____

_____

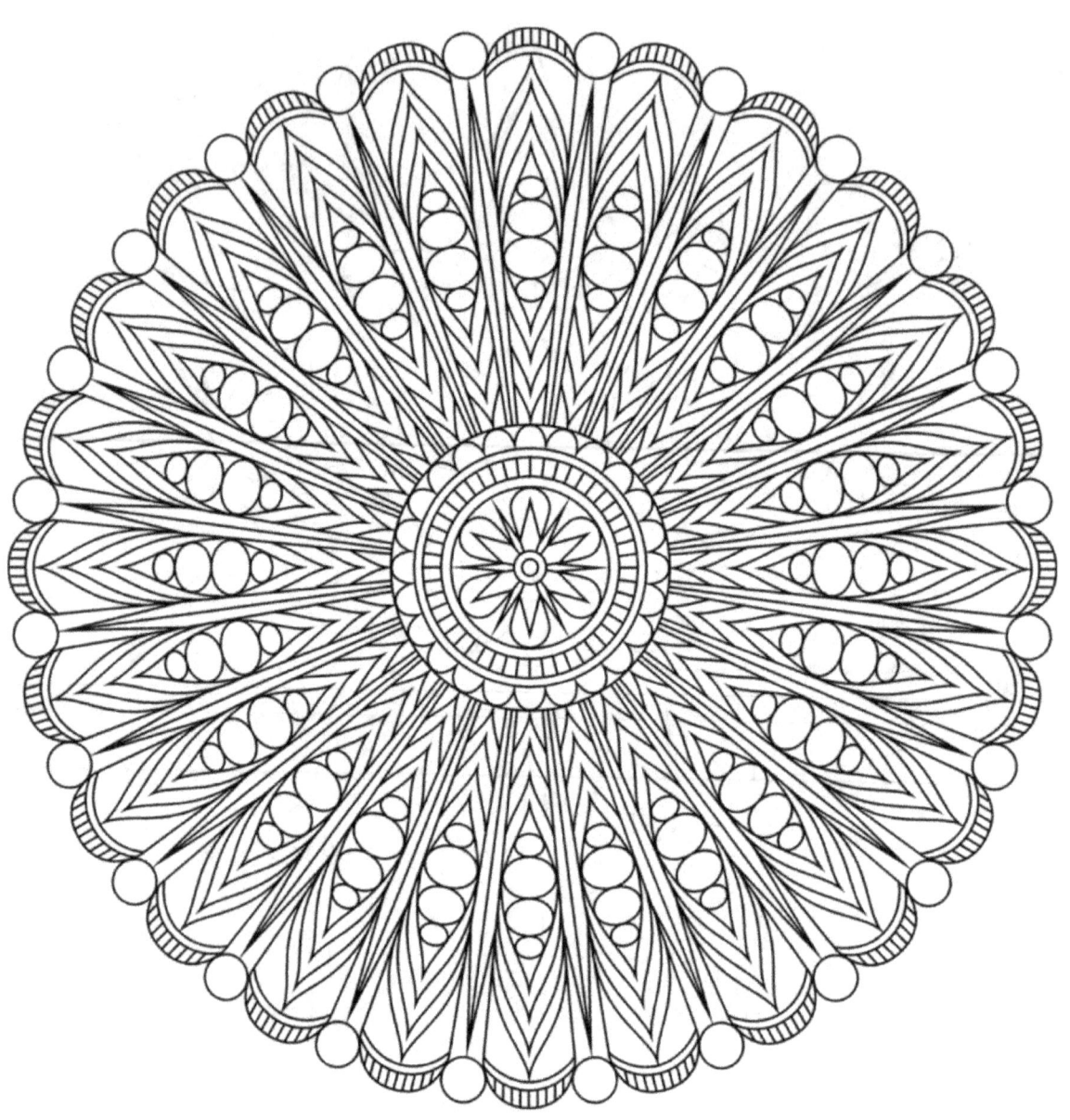

"The best way to cheer yourself is to try to cheer someone else up." - Mark Twain

Today I am grateful for

_____

_____

_____

_____

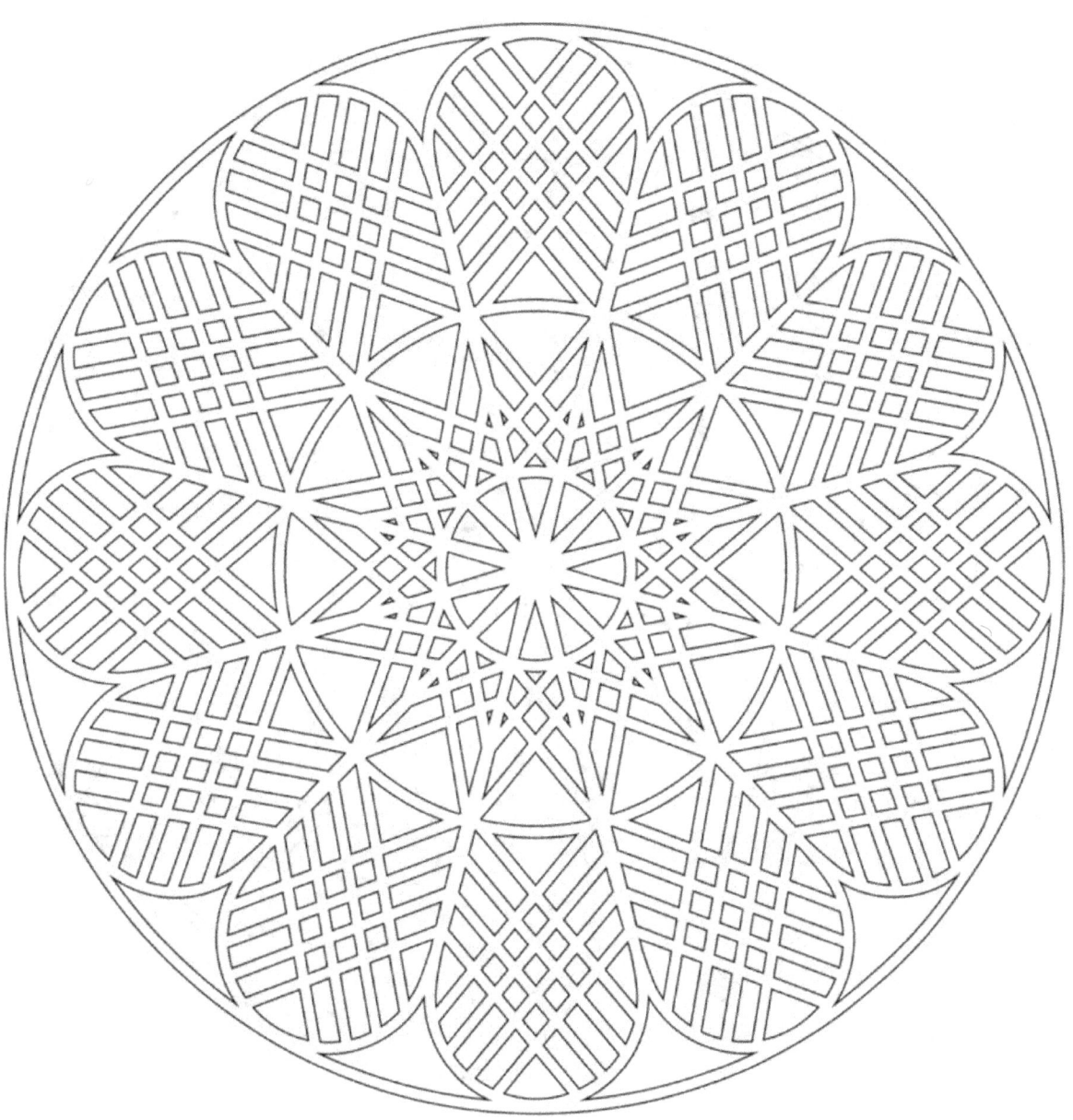

"Don't cry because it's over, smile because it happened." - Dr. Seuss

Today I am grateful for _____

_____

_____

_____

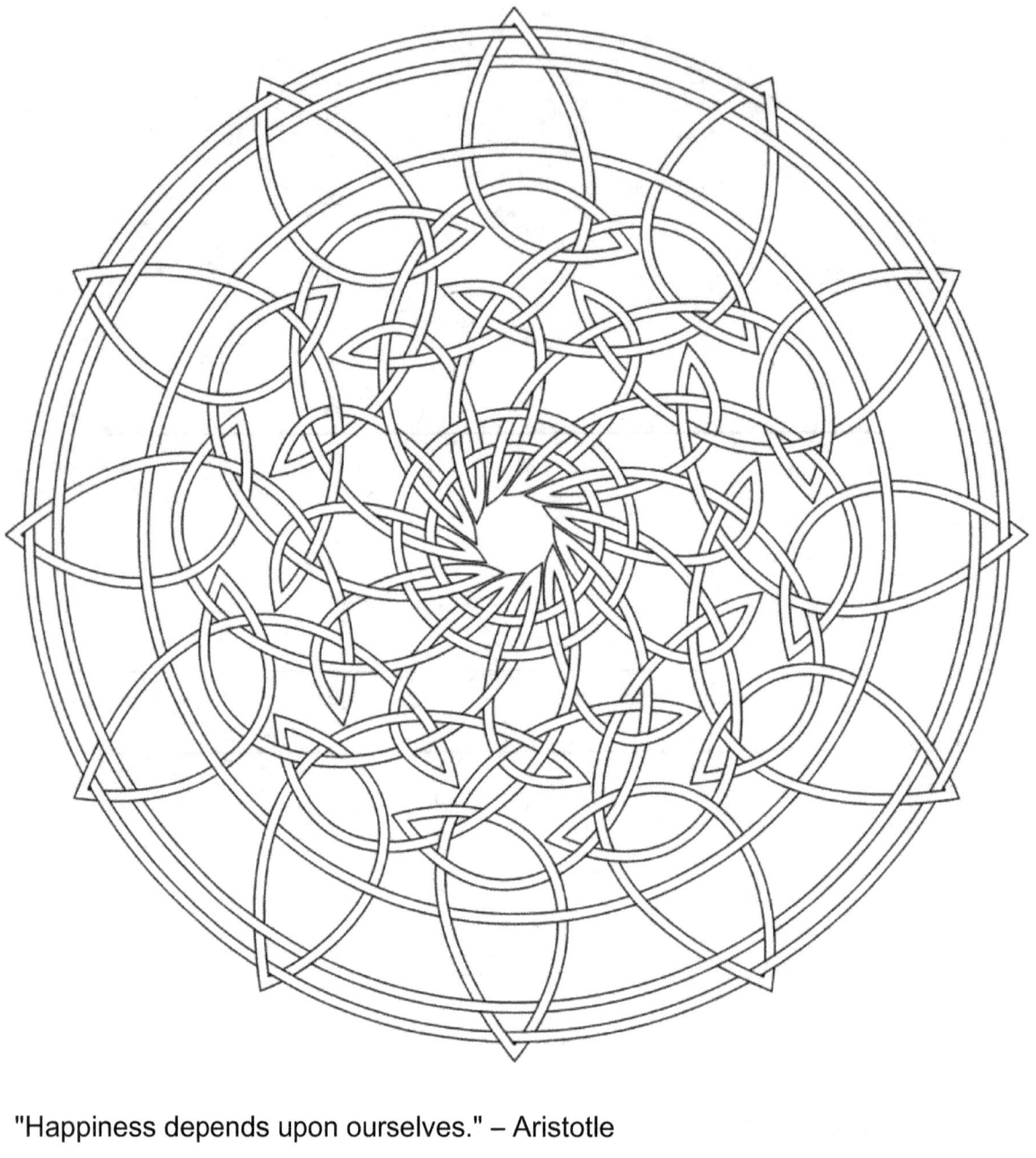

"Happiness depends upon ourselves." – Aristotle

Today I am grateful for

_____

_____

_____

_____

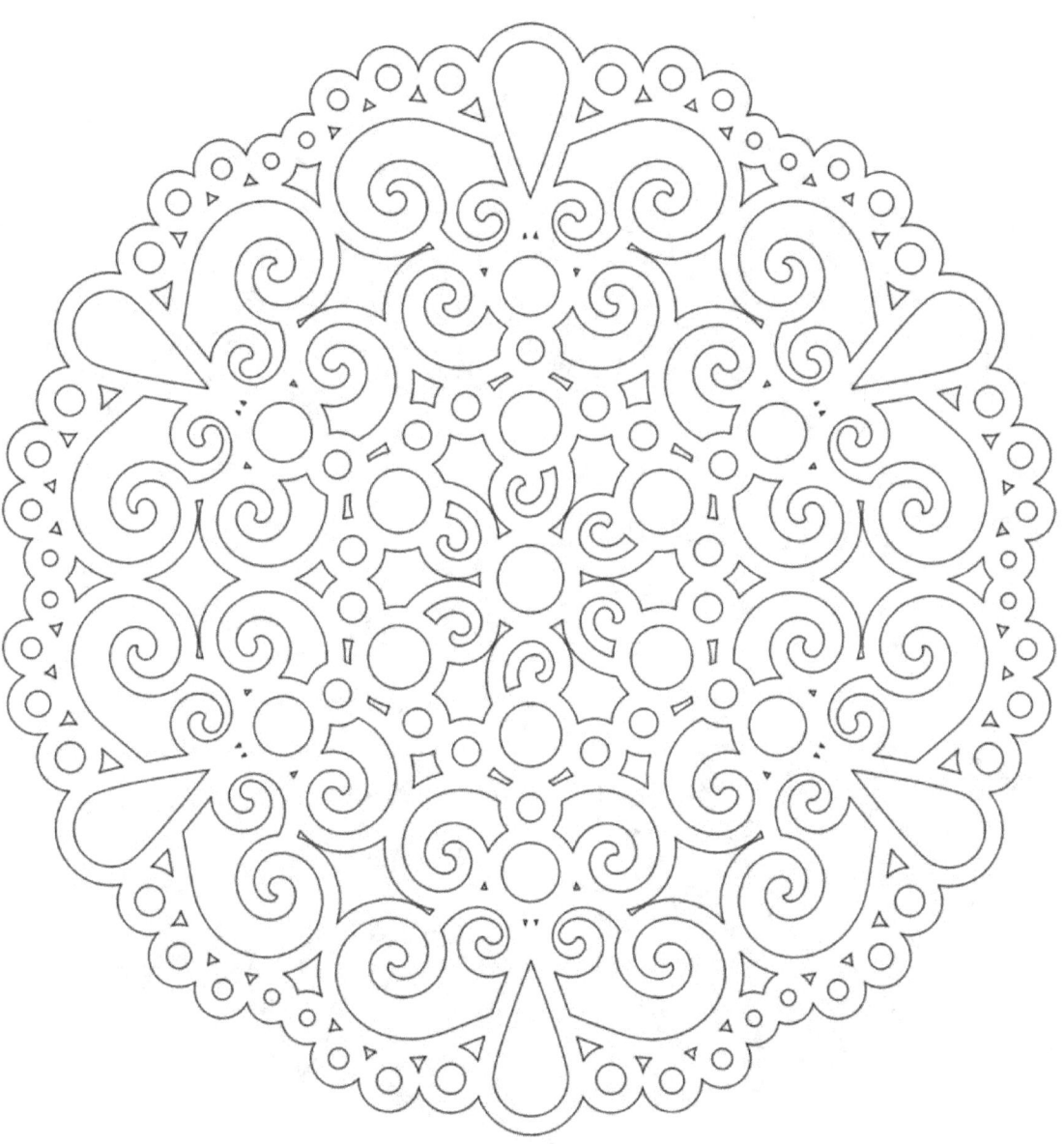

"Happiness cannot be traveled to, owned, earned, worn or consumed. Happiness is the spiritual experience of living every minute with love, grace, and gratitude" - Denis Waitley

Today I am grateful for _____

_____

_____

_____

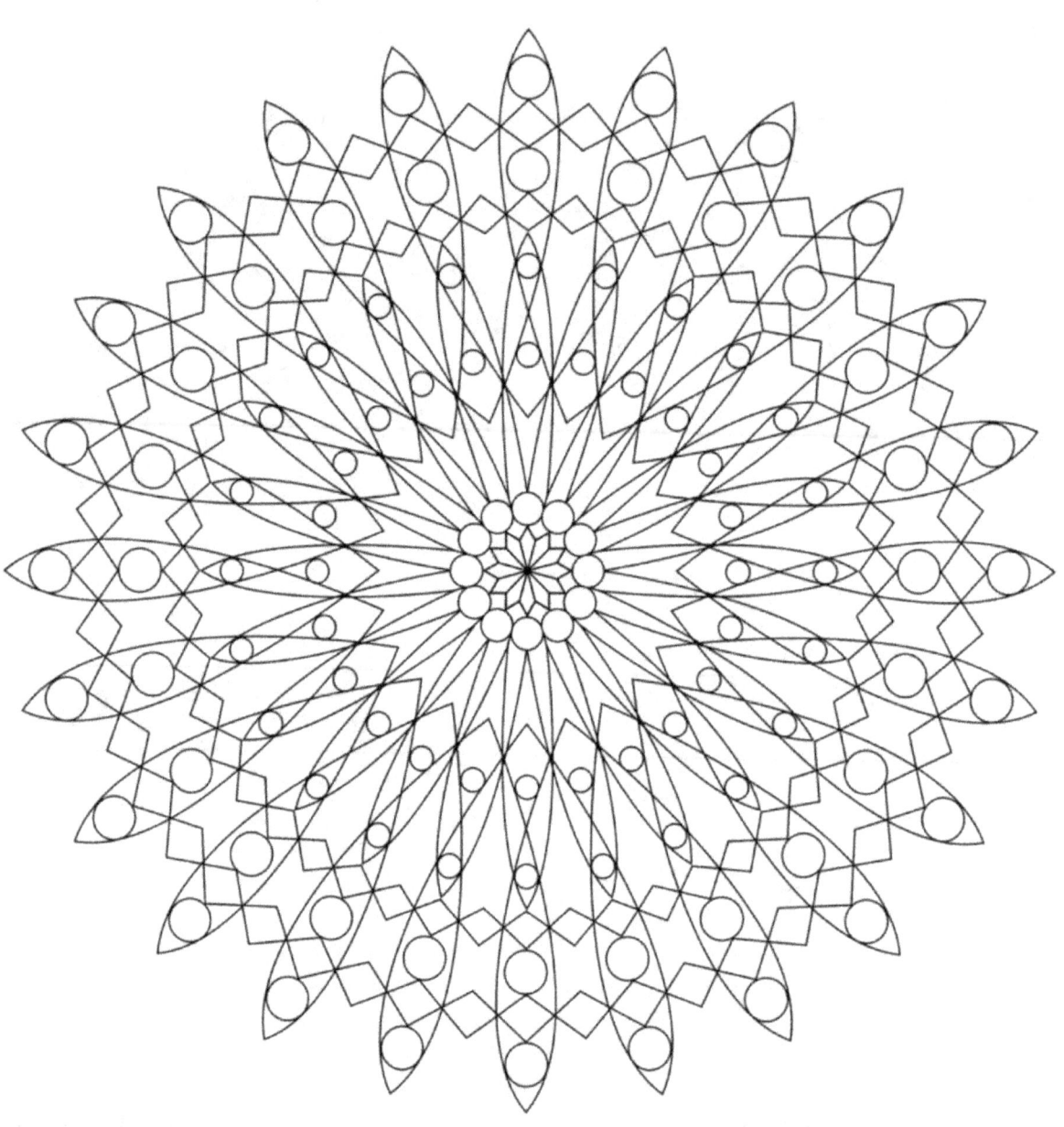

"Some cause happiness wherever they go; others whenever they go."- Oscar Wilde

Today I am grateful for _____

_____

_____

_____

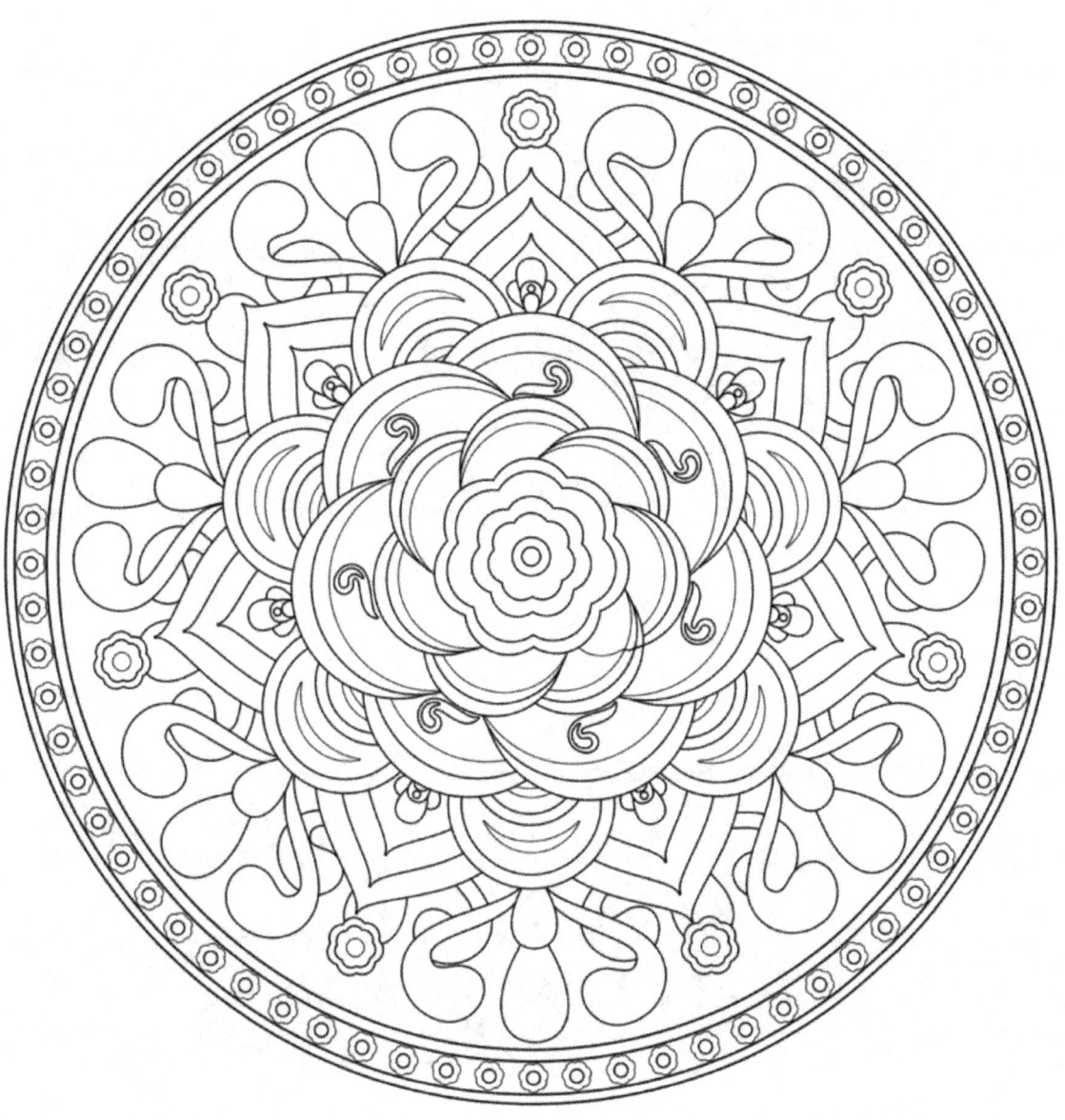

"Be healthy and take care of yourself, but be happy with the beautiful things that make you, you." – Beyoncé

Today I am grateful for _____

_____

_____

_____

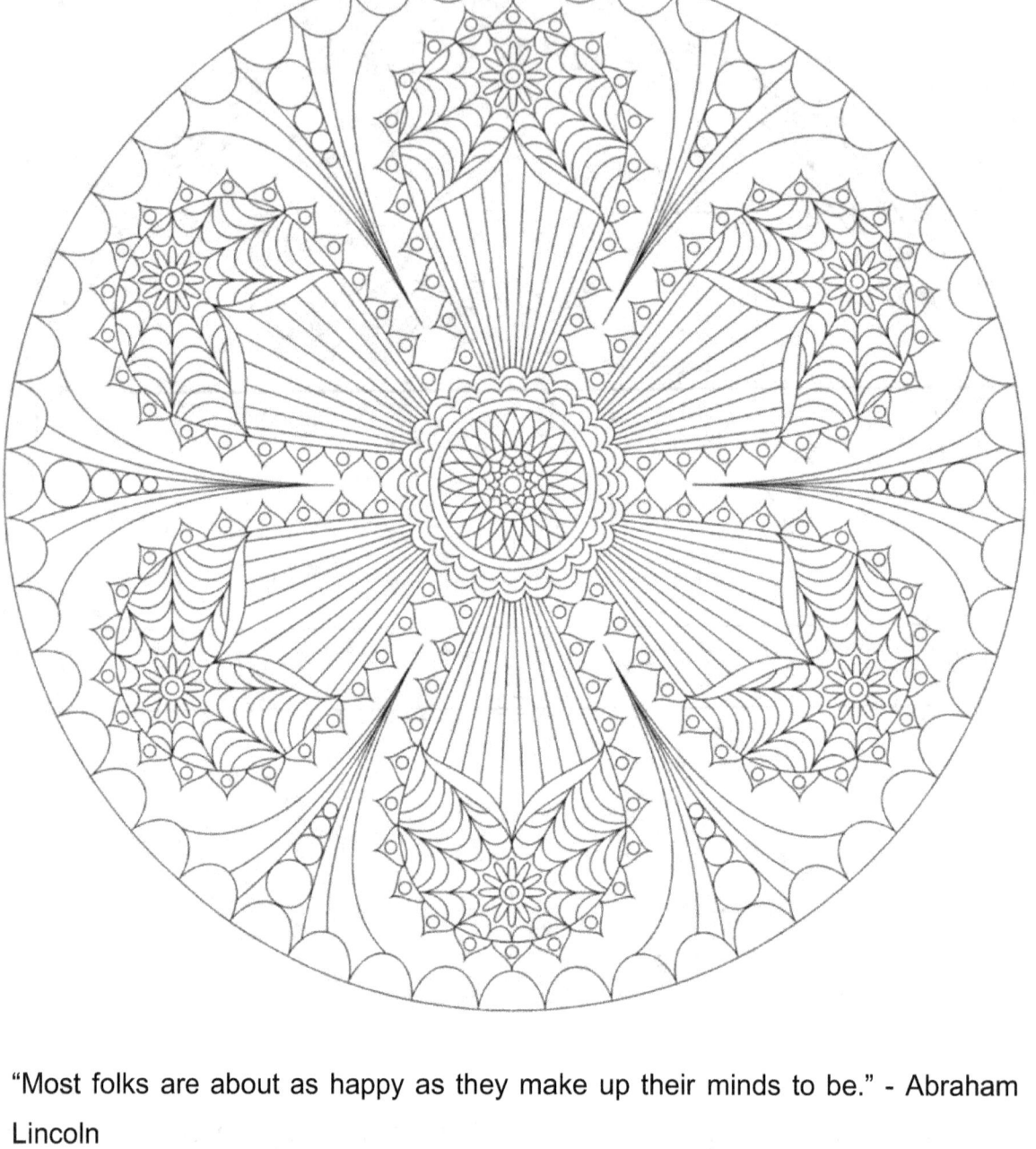

"Most folks are about as happy as they make up their minds to be." - Abraham Lincoln

Today I am grateful for _____

_____

_____

_____

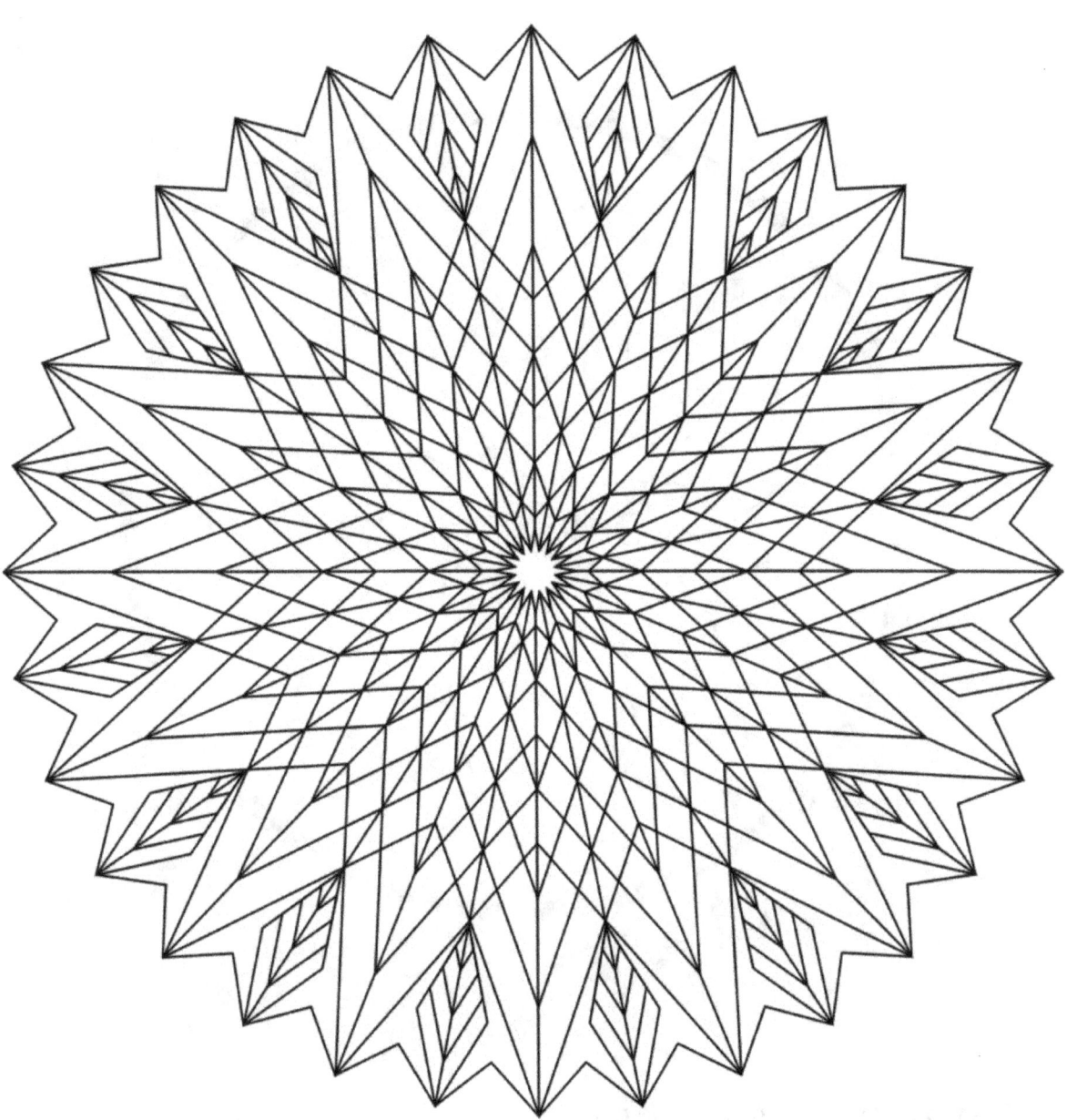

"For every minute you are angry you lose sixty seconds of happiness." - Ralph Waldo Emerson

Today I am grateful for _____

_____

_____

_____

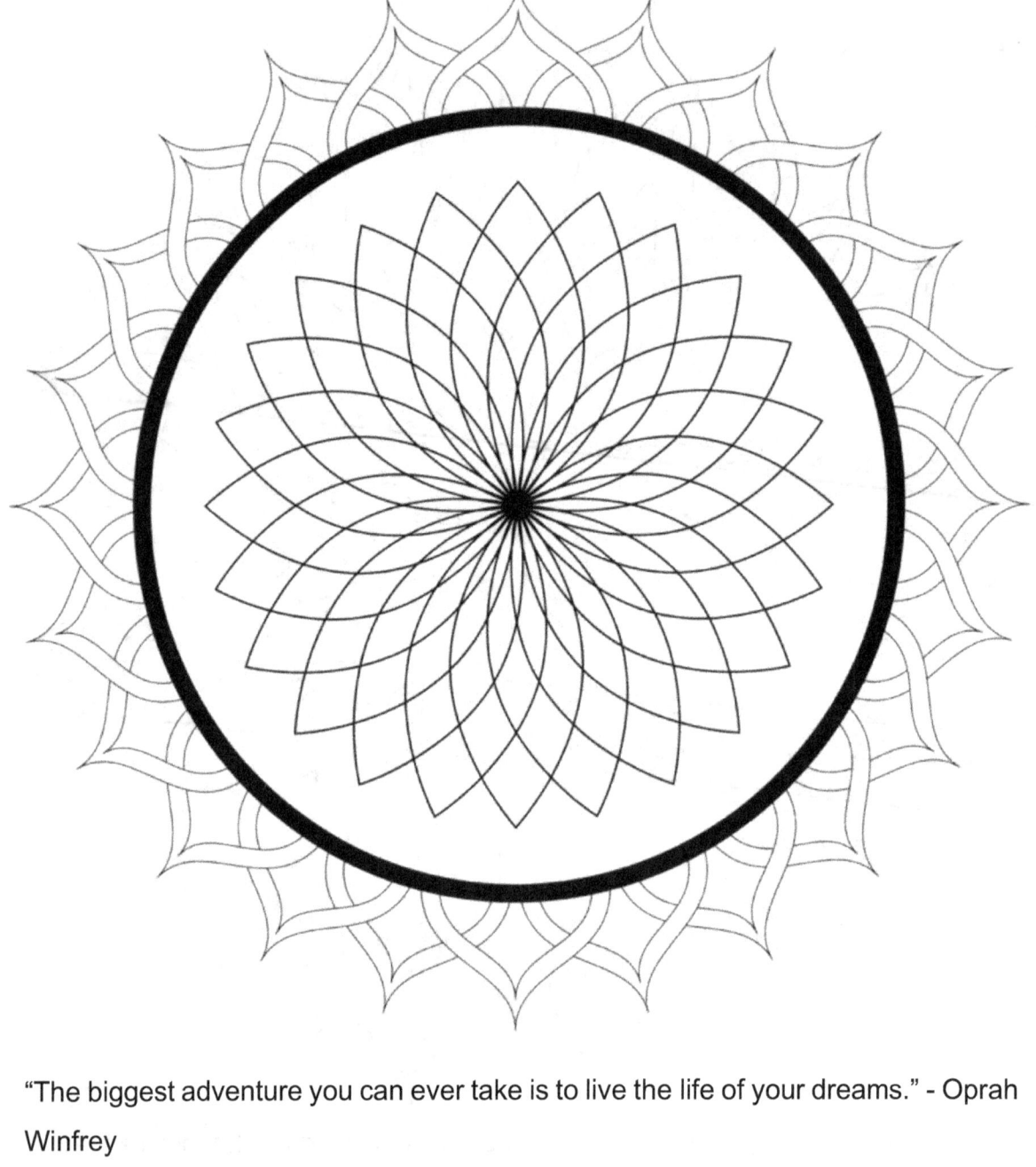

"The biggest adventure you can ever take is to live the life of your dreams." - Oprah Winfrey

Today I am grateful for _____

_____

_____

_____

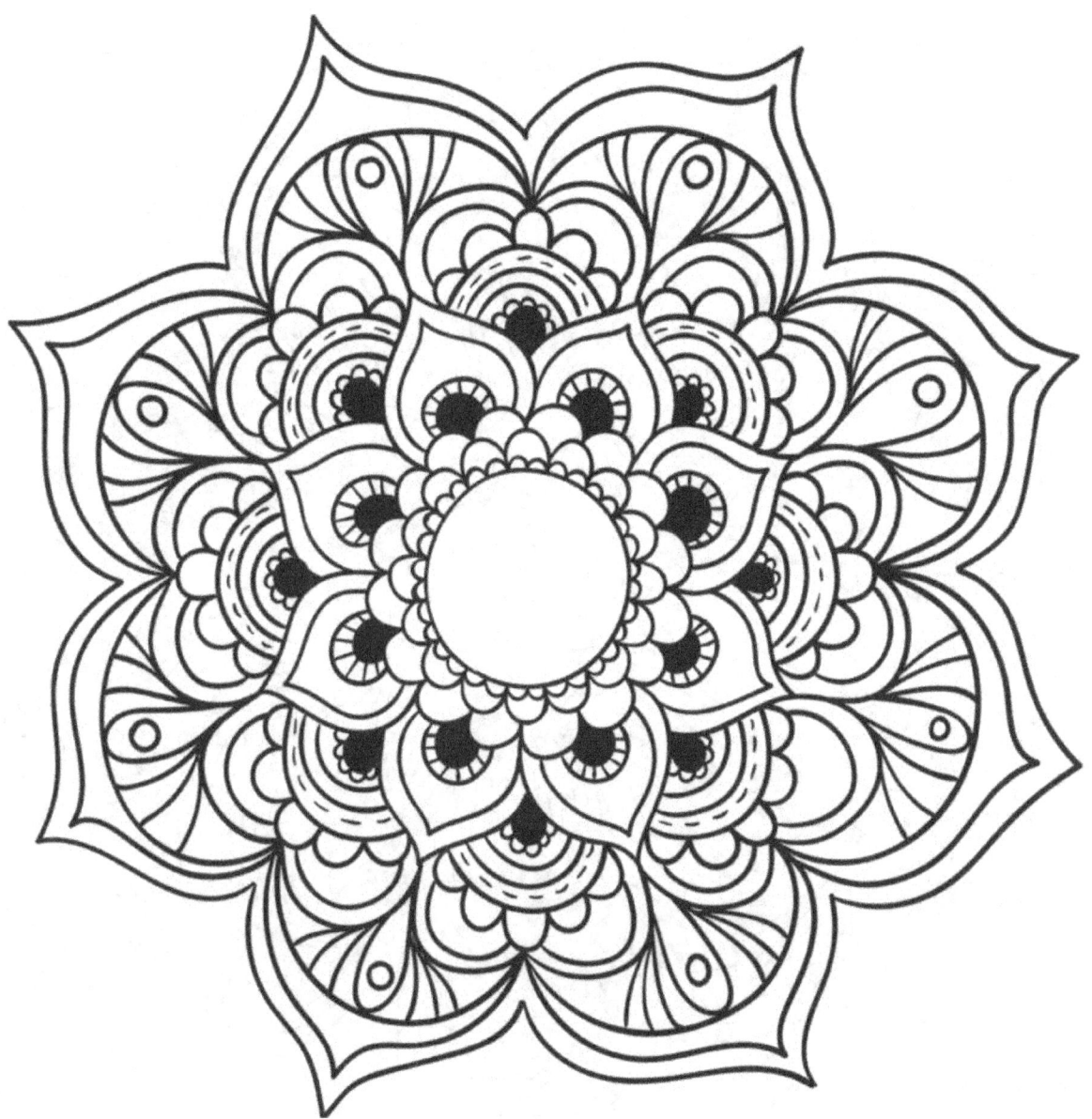

"Everything has its wonders, even darkness and silence, and I learn, whatever state I may be in, therein to be content."- Helen Keller

Today I am grateful for _____

_____

_____

_____

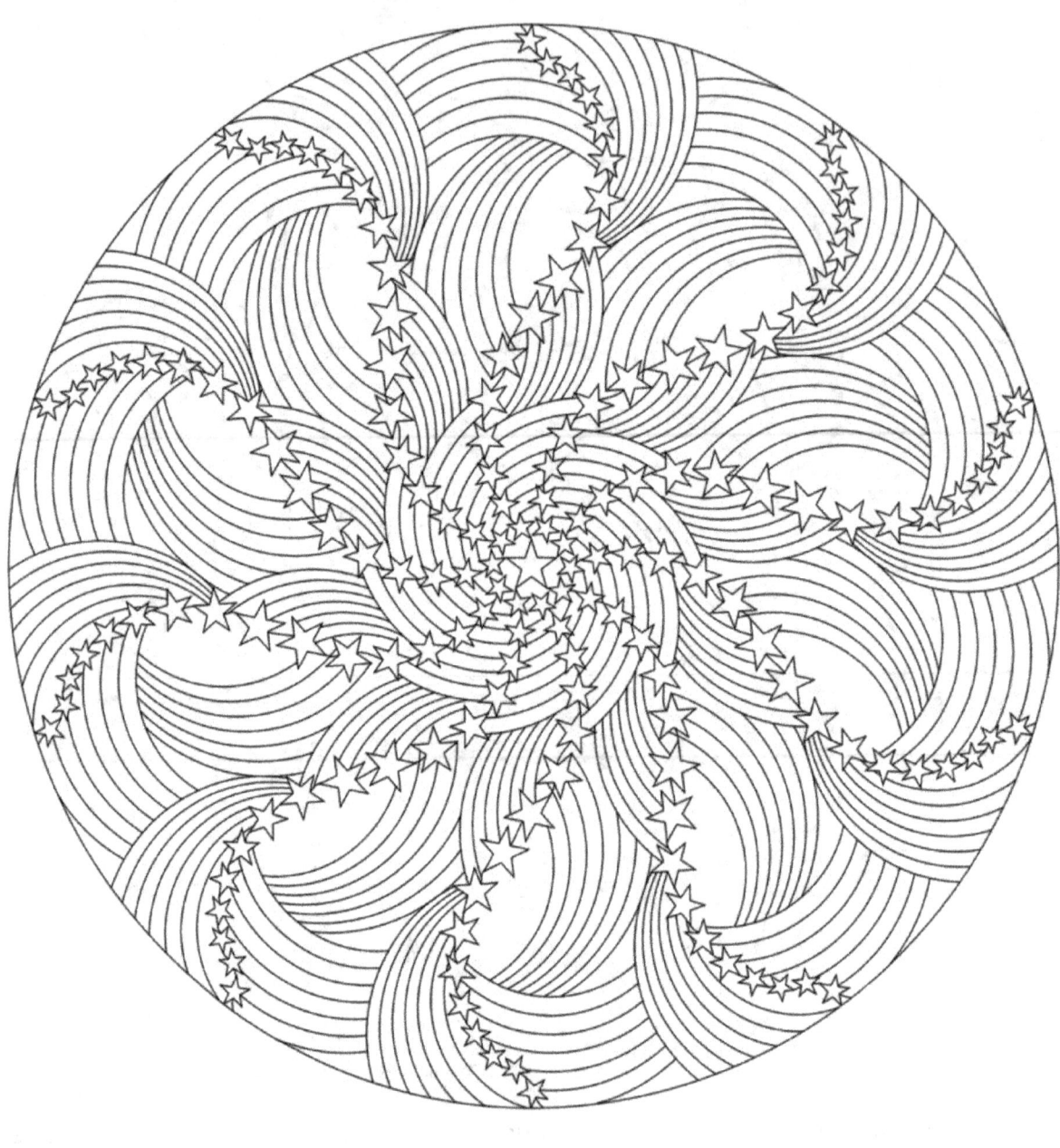

"There is only one way to happiness and that is to cease worrying about things which are beyond the power of our will." – Epictetus

Today I am grateful for _____

_____

_____

_____

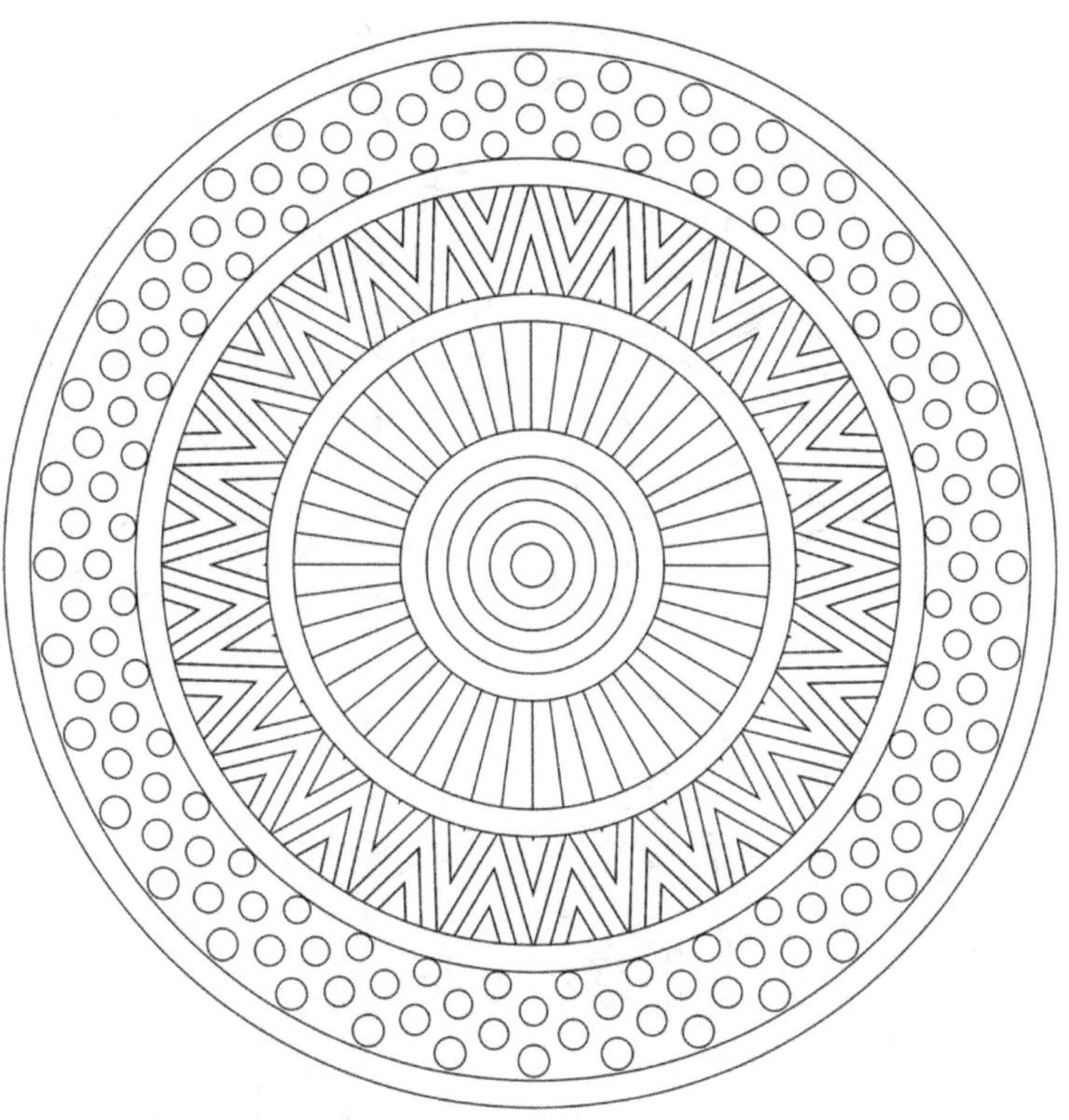

"Cry. Forgive. Learn. Move on. Let your tears water the seeds of your future happiness." - Steve Marabol

Today I am grateful for _____

_____

_____

_____

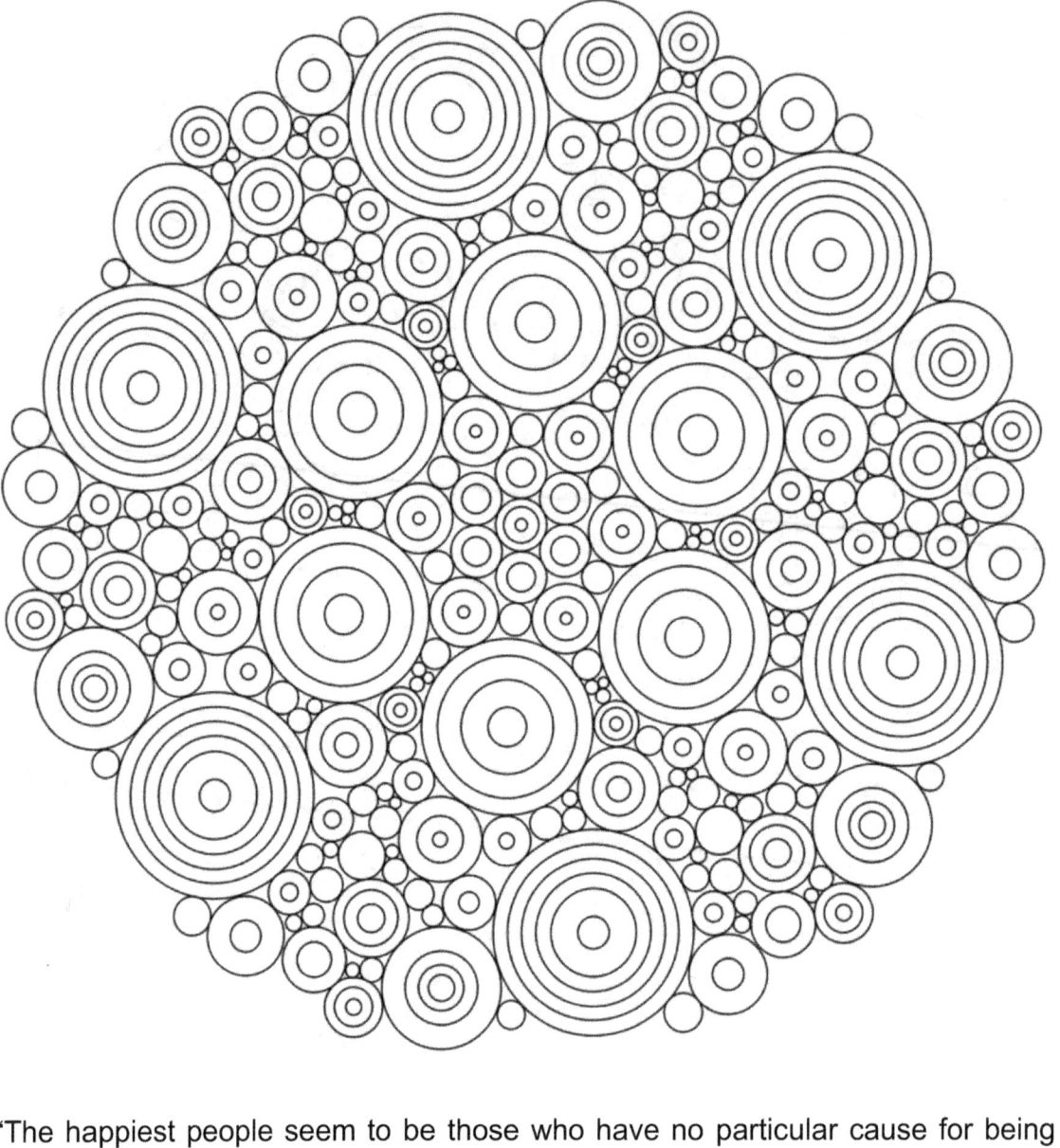

"The happiest people seem to be those who have no particular cause for being happy except that they are so." - William Ralph Inge

Today I am grateful for _____

_____

_____

_____

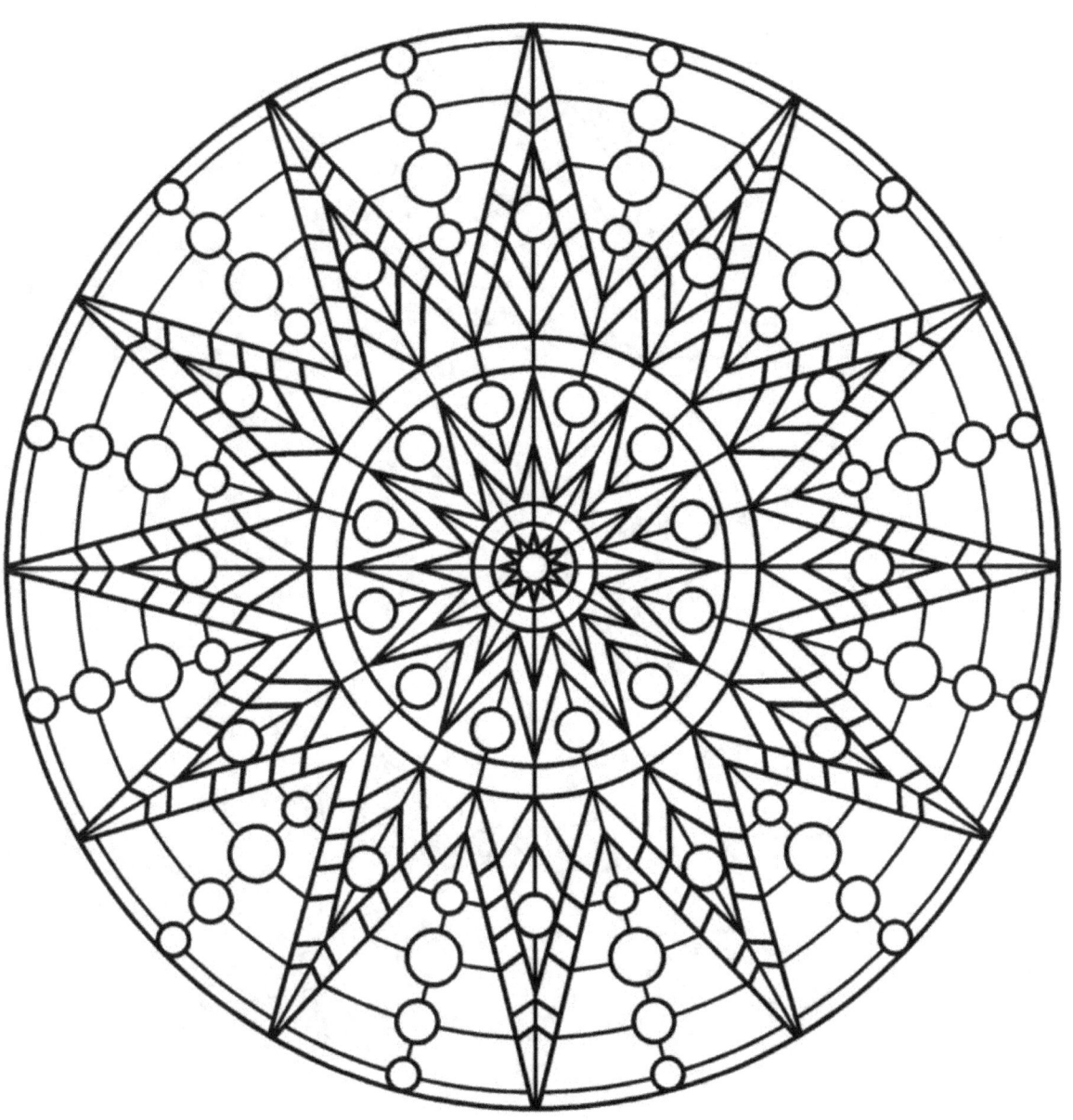

"Beauty is everywhere. You only have to look to see it." -Bob Ross

Today I am grateful for _____

_____

_____

_____

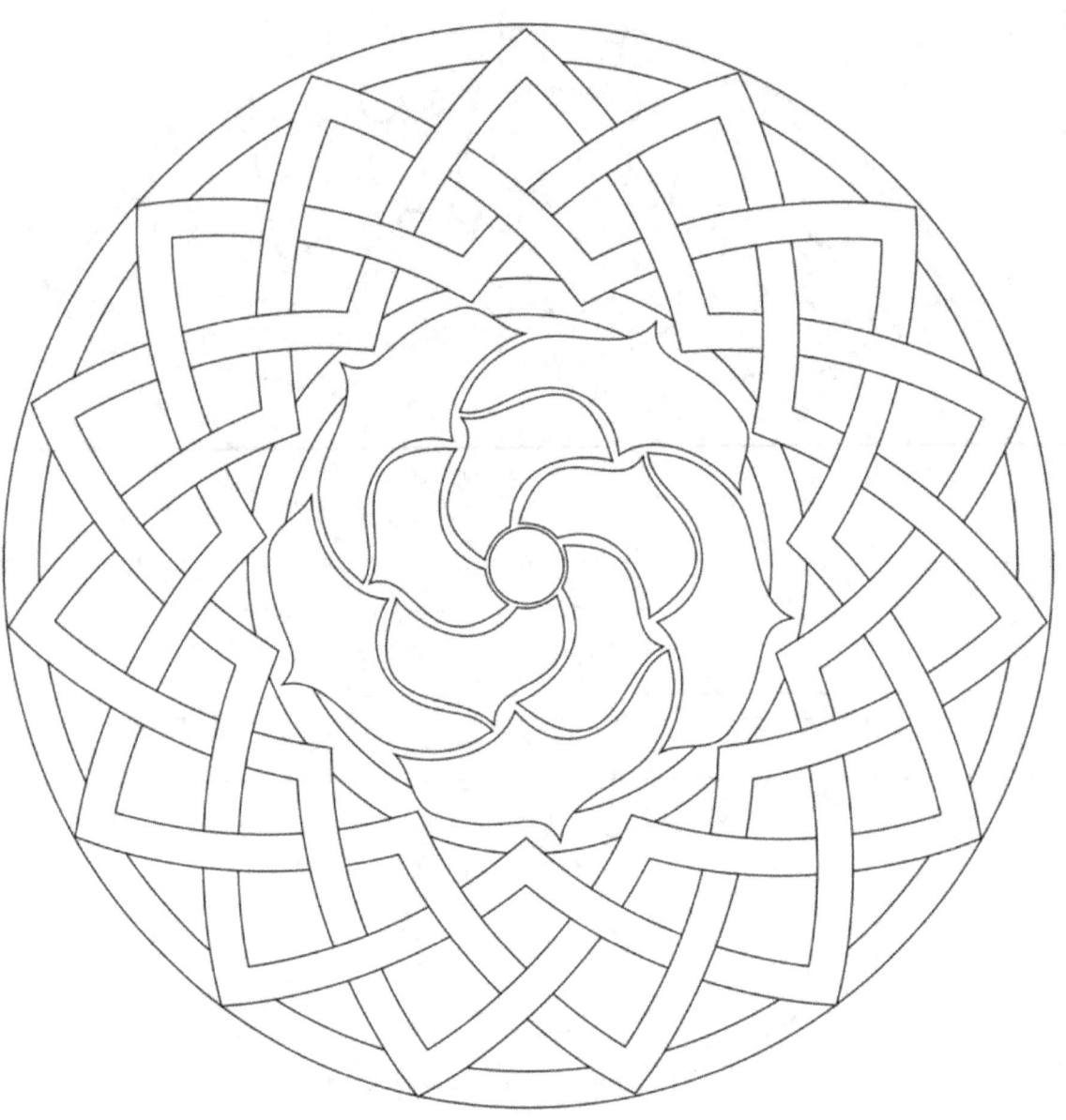

"Life is the dancer and you are the dance." - Eckhart Tolle

Today I am grateful for _____

_____

_____

_____

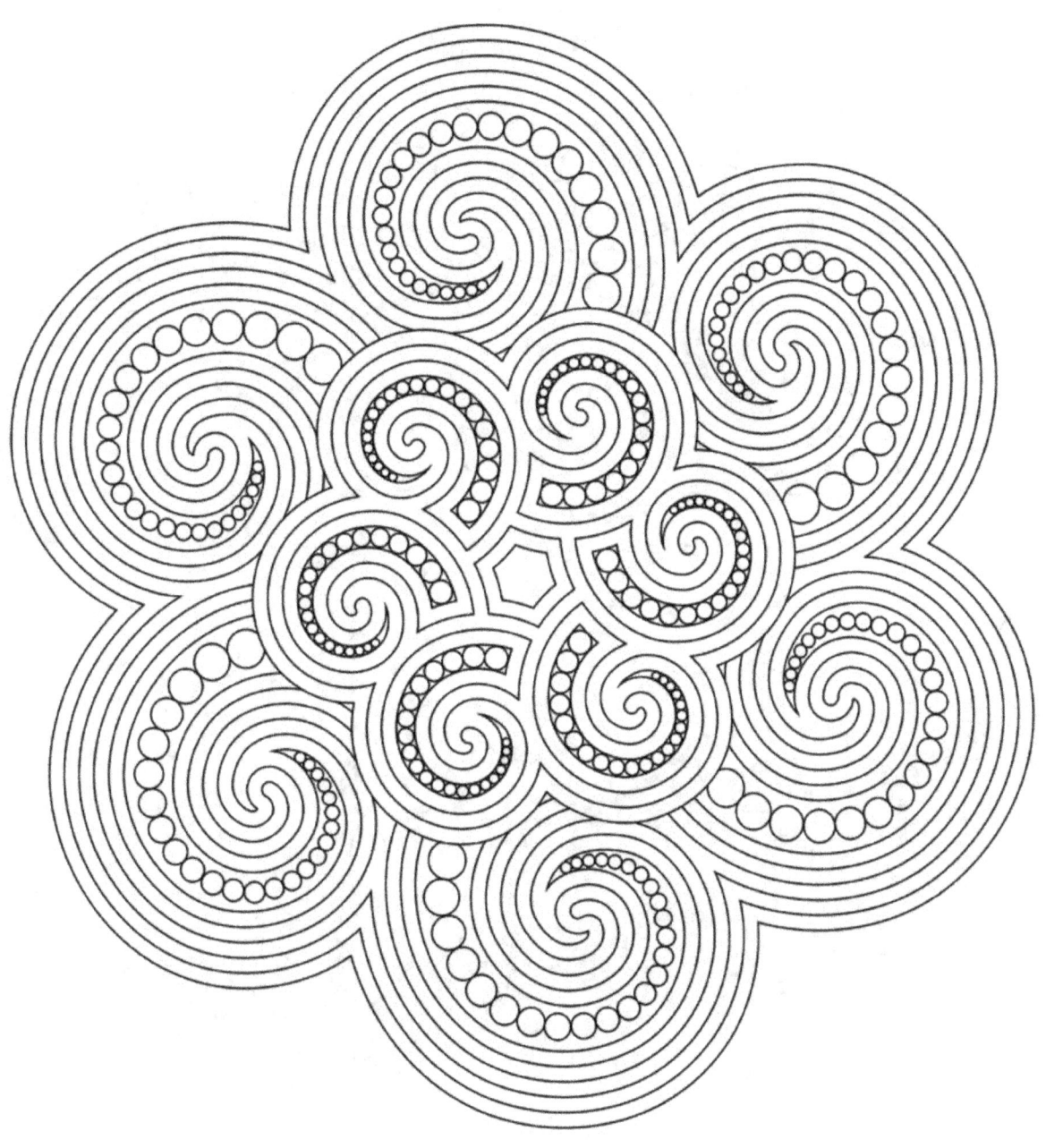

"The point is not to pay back kindness but to pass it on." - Julia Alvarez

Today I am grateful for

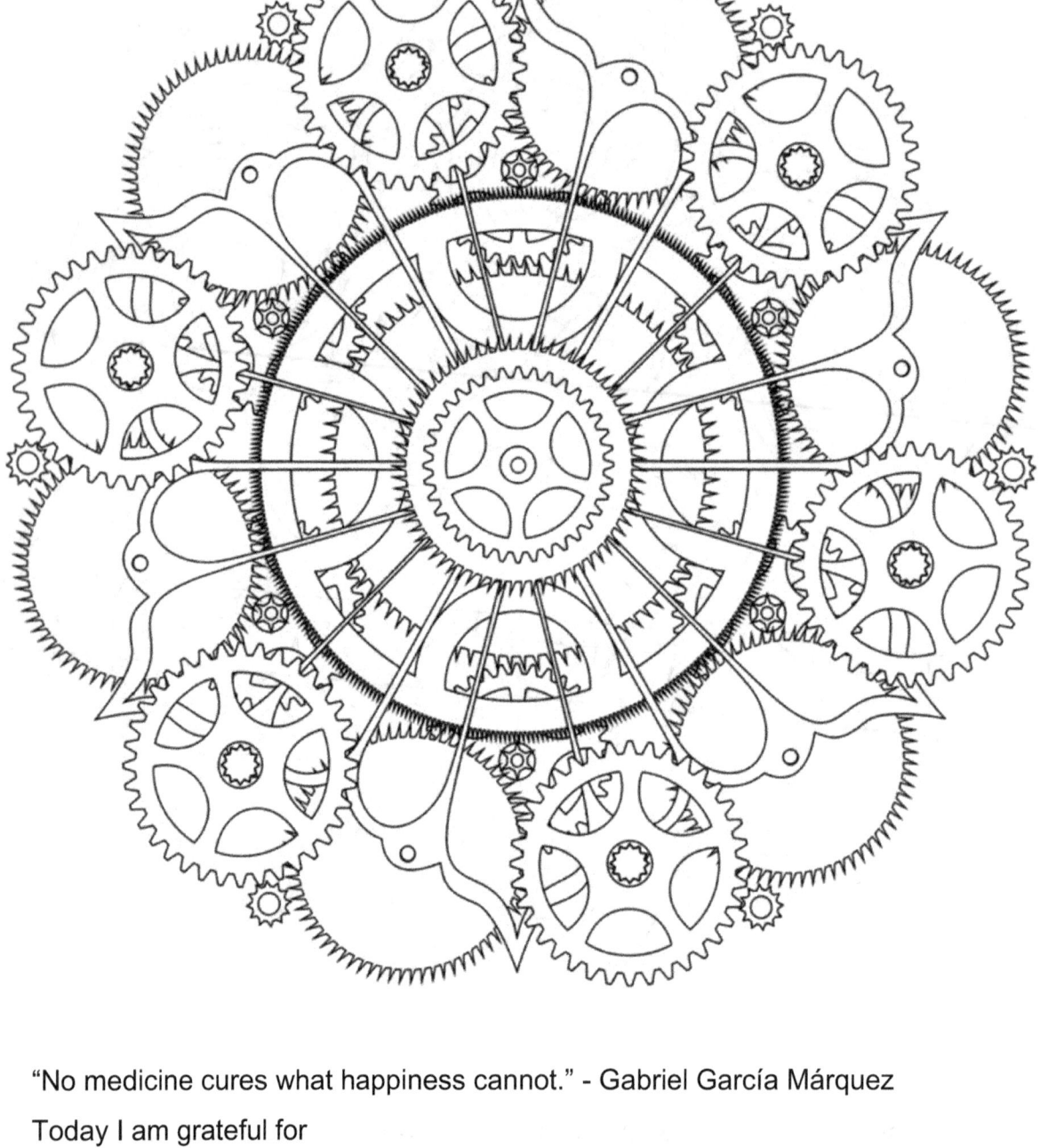

"No medicine cures what happiness cannot." - Gabriel García Márquez

Today I am grateful for _____

_____

_____

_____

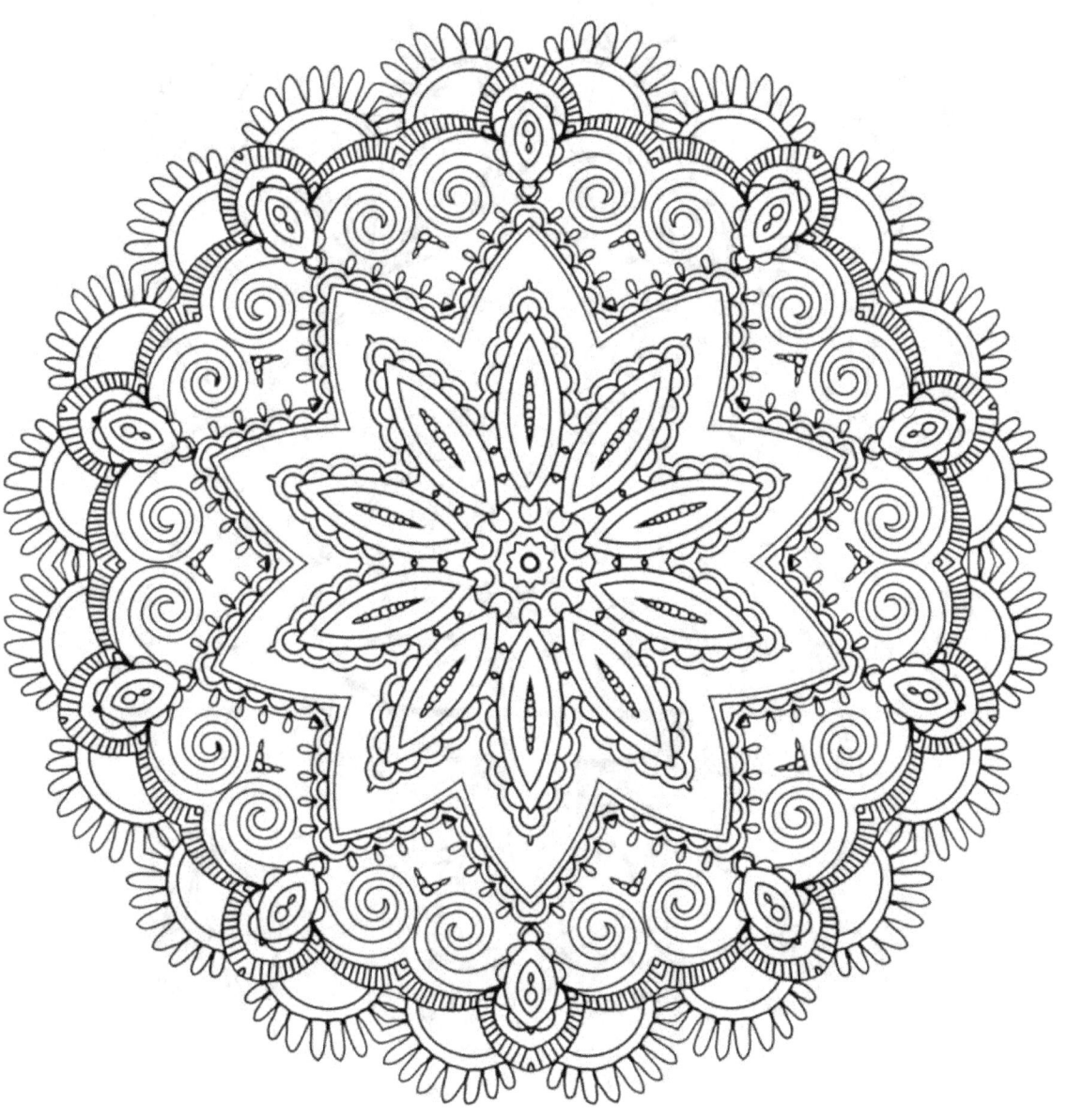

"If you have only one smile in you give it to the people you love." - Maya Angelou

Today I am grateful for _____

_____

_____

_____

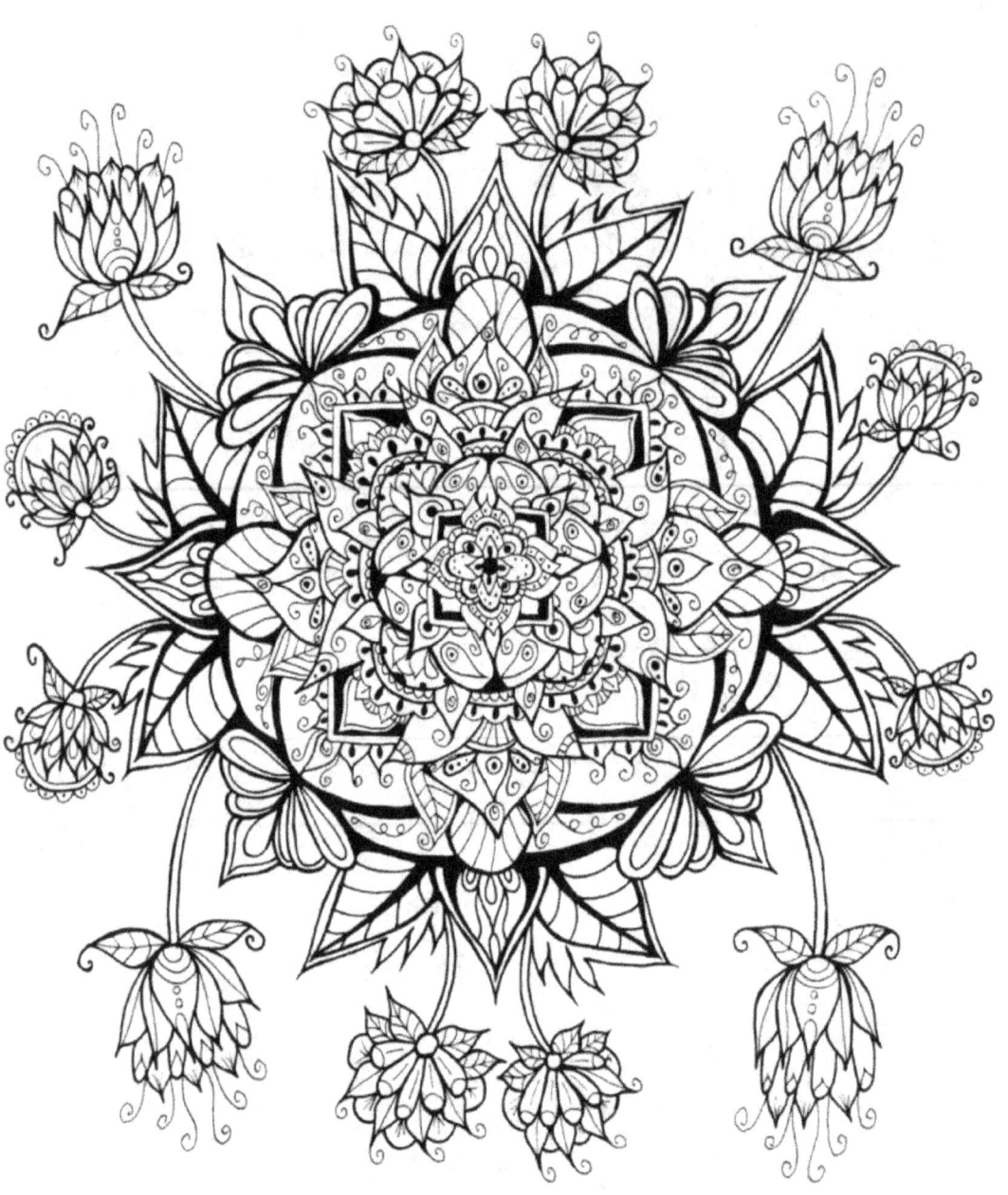

"Let us be grateful to the people who make us happy; they are the charming gardeners who make our souls blossom." - Marcel Proust

Today I am grateful for _____

_____

_____

_____

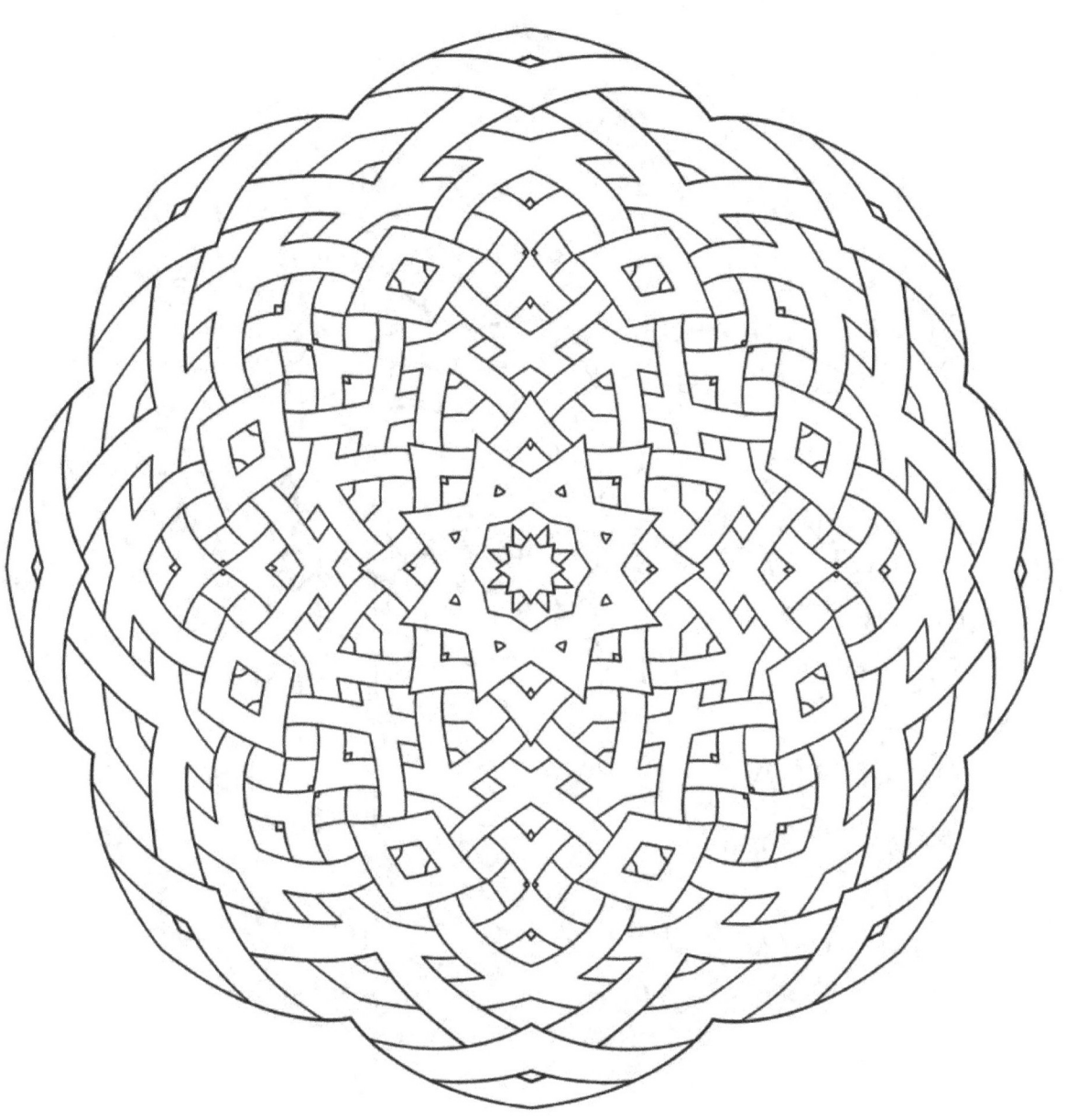

"You cannot protect yourself from sadness without protecting yourself from happiness." - Jonathan Safran Foer

Today I am grateful for _____

_____

_____

_____

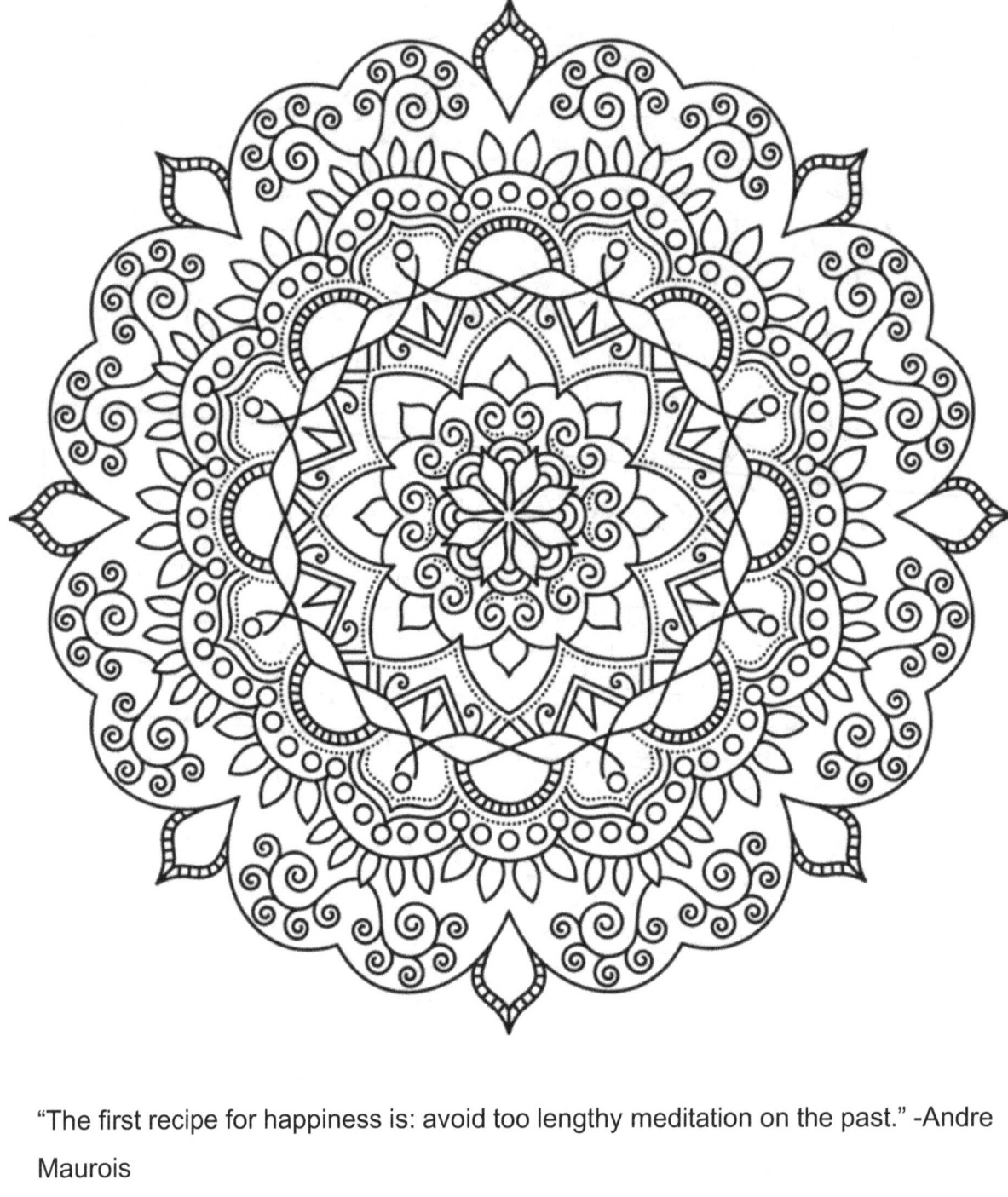

"The first recipe for happiness is: avoid too lengthy meditation on the past." -Andre Maurois

Today I am grateful for

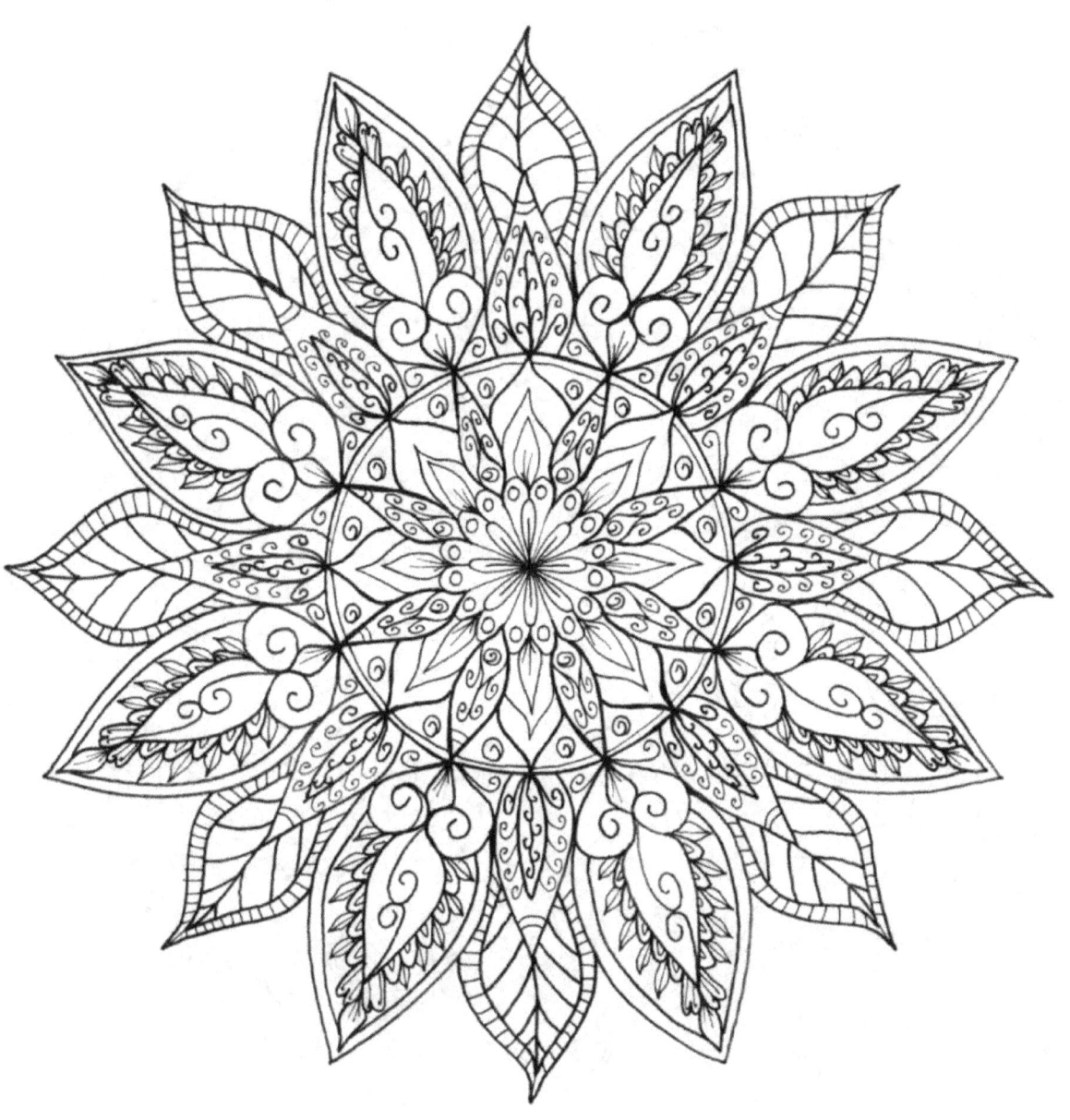

"Even a happy life cannot be without a measure of darkness, and the word happy would lose its meaning if it were not balanced by sadness. It is far better to take things as they come along with patience and equanimity." - Carl Jung

Today I am grateful for _____

_____

_____

_____

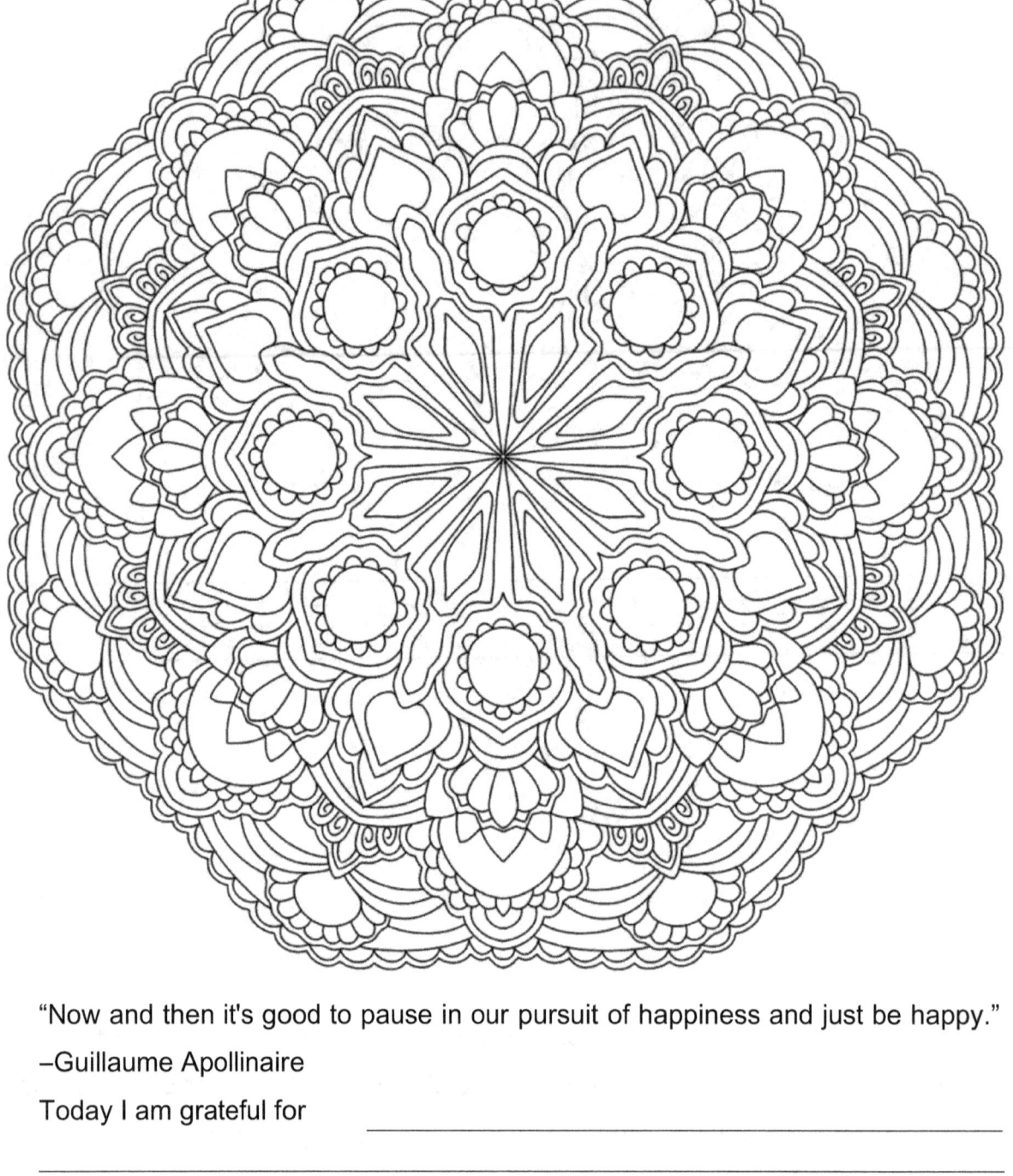

"Now and then it's good to pause in our pursuit of happiness and just be happy."

–Guillaume Apollinaire

Today I am grateful for

_____

_____

_____

_____

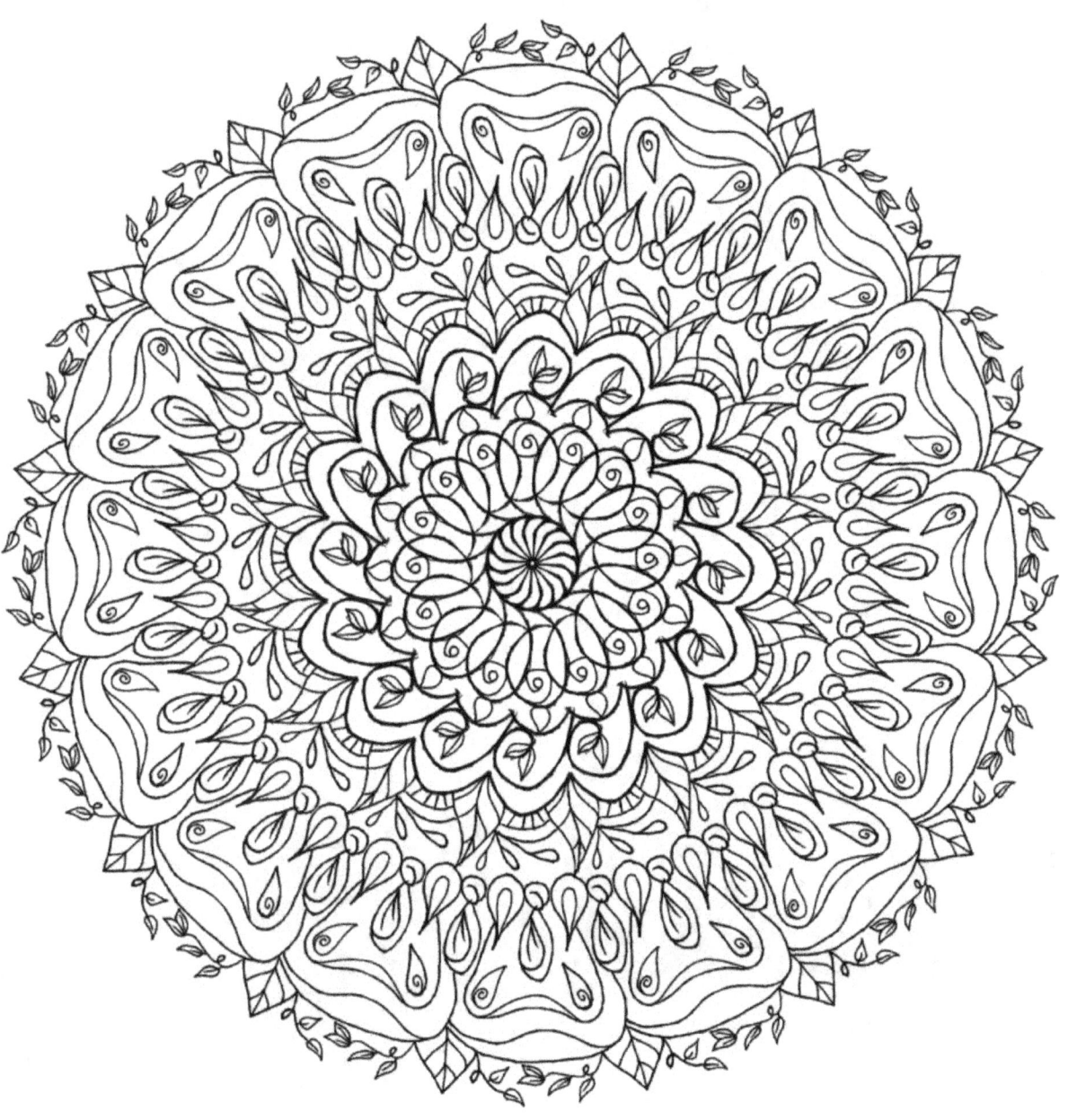

"Happiness is not the absence of problems, it's the ability to deal with them." –Steve Maraboli

Today I am grateful for
_____

_____

_____

_____

"I'm choosing happiness over suffering, I know I am. I'm making space for the unknown future to fill up my life with yet-to-come surprises." –Elizabeth Gilbert

Today I am grateful for _____

_____

_____

_____

"Action may not always bring happiness, but there is no happiness without action.
" –William James

Today I am grateful for _____

_____

_____

_____

"Happiness is a risk. If you're not a little scared, then you're not doing it right."

–Sarah Addison Allen

Today I am grateful for _____

_____

_____

_____

"Happiness is a perfume you cannot pour on others without getting some on yourself." –Ralph Waldo Emerson

Today I am grateful for _____

_____

_____

_____

"Happiness is like those palaces in fairytales whose gates are guarded by dragons: We must fight in order to conquer it." –Alexandre Dumas

Today I am grateful for _____

_____

_____

_____

"It is necessary to the happiness of man that he be mentally faithful to himself. Infidelity does not consist in believing, or in disbelieving, it consists in professing to believe what he does not believe." –Thomas Paine

Today I am grateful for _____

_____

_____

_____

"Happiness doesn't come from achievements, or money, or any sort of treasure. Happiness is a frame of mind, not a destination. It's appreciating what you've got and building relationships with those around you." –Janette Rallison

Today I am grateful for _____

_____

_____

_____

"Happiness comes from living as you need to, as you want to. As your inner voice tells you to. Happiness comes from being who you actually are instead of who you think you are supposed to be." —Shonda Rhimes

Today I am grateful for _____

_____

_____

_____

"One is happy as a result of one's own efforts once one knows the necessary ingredients of happiness: simple tastes, a certain degree of courage, self-denial to a point, love of work, and above all, a clear conscience." –George Sand

Today I am grateful for _____

_____

_____

_____

Just because you are happy it does not mean that the day is perfect but that you have looked beyond its imperfections" –Bob Marley

Today I am grateful for _____

_____

_____

_____

Mandala: a way of relaxing meditation